Amazing Faith

Spirit-filled messages from
across America, offering hope
that comes from trusting God in
troubled times.

INSIGHT PUBLISHING
SEVIERVILLE, TENNESSEE

© 2007 by Insight Publishing Company.

Disclaimer: This book is a compilation of ideas from numerous experts who have each contributed a chapter. As such, the views expressed in each chapter are of those who were featured and not necessarily of Insight Publishing.

Published by Insight Publishing Company
P.O. Box 4189
Sevierville, Tennessee 37864

10 9 8 7 6 5 4 3 2

Printed in the United States of America

ISBN10: 1-60013- 157-3
ISBN13: 1-60013-157-8

Table of Contents

A Message from the Publisher

This unusual book contains unforgettable stories told by several people who have experienced defining moments that forever changed them and made their faith truly amazing.

One can learn remarkable things when one's faith is tried. From personal experience I can tell you that this is true. Several years ago my wife was diagnosed with cancer. I'll have to say that I learned more about faith during that time than in all the many years I've served as a church staff member and in the music ministry. We struggled and asked all the usual questions people ask in similar circumstances. Now that we're on the other side and my wife is thankfully well, we realize how much our faith grew as a result of our experience with adversity.

As you read the stories in this book, keep in mind that these folks are basically just everyday people who had extraordinary encounters with a living God whose love was revealed in ways sometimes difficult to understand. Trials and times of testing can be vital catalysts for change and growth. When these authors were tested they found that God truly was an "... ever present help in trouble" (Psalm 46:1 KJV). They discovered that there is a decided difference between joy *because of* trials, and joy *in spite* of trials.

I cannot help but marvel at the courage and perseverance of these authors who have traveled the path of adversity. I hope you too will be inspired and encouraged as you read these stories of faith tested—faith developed—faith made amazing.

Interviews conducted by:
David E. Wright
President, International Speakers Network

Rhonda Jones

A mazing faith—just the phrase conjures thoughts of renowned theologians of our day or the great men and women immortalized in the Bible. My own personal experience has been quite different.

My youth was spent attending the little Methodist church in the country where my father's family had worshipped for decades. Yet in my adulthood, I had drifted further and further away from regular church attendance or any kind of growing relationship with God. Consciously or unconsciously I had essentially sold my soul to climb the corporate ladder.

By the time I reached my late thirties, it had been a few years since I'd attended church anywhere. So it was unusual for me to even notice the First United Methodist Church of Jefferson City nestled right up against the street I traveled to work each day. Furthermore, as I waited at the stoplight one morning, it startled me to be suddenly overcome by the impulse to attend this church. By the following Sunday I was not only sitting among the group of strangers, but during the time for congregational prayer requests, I asked for prayer for someone completely unknown to them—my cousin Jill.

With the exception of Saturday, we spent almost every day together during the first formative years of our lives. We went to the same school and the same church and spent the summers out of school staying with our grandfather. So, although I have only one sister by birth, Jill and her sister are my sisters too, bound to me by the heartstrings of our shared family experience.

About eleven years before the occurrence of the story I'm about to share with you, Jill had literally almost died with complications from the birth of her first child. When the baby went home from the hospital, Jill did not. She spent several months fighting for her twenty-year-old life, having every possible inch of her colon removed short of a colostomy, and surviving multiple operations and bouts with congestive heart failure. Somehow, over a period of several years, she'd recovered and even managed, with her doctor's precautions, to give birth to another child.

As if surviving that many trials in a young life were not enough, she still had to endure the break-up of her marriage, leaving her alone with two young children. Now, finally, with a career in nursing and a new husband who shared her purpose in healthcare, she wanted desperately to give him a child of his own. And we all wished only the best for them.

When we learned Jill was carrying twins, however, our entire family grew very concerned. And, despite our attempts at optimism, our fears appeared to be coming to fruition when, after she had struggled with the pregnancy for four months, she was put on complete bed rest. The plan of the high-risk pregnancy specialist, to whom her case was assigned, was to try to give the babies as much time to develop as her body could support. He hoped to wait until the last possible moment to deliver them, thus preventing any defects normally associated with premature births.

Shortly after I learned Jill was pregnant, something had begun to eat at me. At first I dismissed it as random thoughts—natural concern for Jill's welfare that occasionally crept into my consciousness. Then it became more frequent. More and more I found myself thinking about Jill, wondering how she was doing and whether she would be all right. Until finally, it became an urging, *"What are you going to do for Jill?"*

It didn't matter where I was—at work, in the grocery store, watching television, driving down the road, standing in line at the post office—that question nagged away at me.

"What are you going to do for Jill?" Strangely, though, there was nothing more. No idea what I should do.

My grandmother suggested we give her a baby shower, but for some reason I wasn't compelled to pursue that idea. I considered going to see her. But now that I lived miles away and the demands of my career had caused us to drift out of one another's daily lives, that wasn't normal behavior for us. What would I say if I did visit her? The last thing I wanted to do was act outside the norm and let her know how worried I was.

I kept trying to put it out of my mind, but it wouldn't go away. Then, with shocking suddenness, another admonition occurred to me.

"Don't wait until it's too late!"

It was like carrying on a conversation with myself.

"What are you going to do for Jill?"

"I went to church and requested prayer for her. I don't know what else to do."

"Don't wait until it's too late!"

Now I was concerned but still clueless; and the mysterious beseeching continued. "What are you going to do for Jill—don't wait until it's too late. . . . " I tried to convince myself it was just an overactive imagination.

I received updates on Jill's condition through my mother and grandmother, while I continued to attend my new church. Although I felt increasingly more at home there, since that first Sunday when I'd surprisingly requested prayer for Jill, I'd resigned to praying silently for her and her babies.

One Sunday, right before the start of the service, I noticed a little blurb in the church bulletin: *The Joyful Noises need enthusiastic voices! You don't have to be a professional. Just come to practice on Tuesday at seven in the evening.* It listed two contact names, neither of which I'd ever heard before.

Although I hadn't sung anywhere in years, I couldn't stop looking at that message throughout the service. I felt as compelled by it as I had been initially to attend the church. So on my way out that day I approached one of the ushers and asked him about "The Joyful Noises." He only knew it was some kind of singing group but said he would have someone call me. By the time I arrived home, however, I'd convinced myself I couldn't do it. *What was I thinking? I'm too busy, and it's been too long since I've done anything like this. I'm just not ready. Even if someone calls me, I'm not going to do it.*

When the call came, it was from the wife of a man retired from my company. I knew him well, which caused me to feel by default that I knew her, and both of them also sang in the group. Everything she said was exactly what I needed to hear. I fell right into talking with her about it and any thoughts of backing out vanished. The things she said seemed tailored specifically to me, not the least of which was the reason they put the request in the bulletin—they needed sopranos, which was the part I could sing.

Unfortunately, when the next Tuesday rolled around I had to work late. I finally left the office at nine o'clock having missed practice. I knew the group was going to be rehearsing for the upcoming Easter service. Given the short timeframe, I realized I'd missed a crucial practice if I intended to really do this thing. Now I had another excuse to just drop the whole idea.

Nevertheless, when the next Tuesday rolled around, I couldn't stop thinking about it all day long. So at seven o'clock, I walked into the practice room in a part of the church I'd never seen before, with people I'd never met, to quickly learn that not only were we practicing songs for the Easter service, but we would be singing this coming Sunday—five songs I'd never even heard before! For the first time in a long time, my knees were weak, and I was sick at my stomach. With one hour of practice under my belt, I was dreading Sunday morning already. I barely had an idea how the songs went. I couldn't believe I had added this extra stress to my life.

At the end of practice the ten members of the group gathered with clasped hands in a small circle and each began to talk about what was going on in their lives—family members, friends, or situations—for which they needed emotional or spiritual support. I was a little hesitant, but soon found myself telling them about Jill and the twins. We then prayed together for her and others who had been mentioned. Smiling from ear to ear, I left the church that evening with my spirits uplifted.

I had no more than arrived home when the phone rang. I heard my grandmother struggling through tears on the other end of the line and my spirits sank.

"Jill went into labor," she said, "and both babies died." Her voice broke as she tried to continue.

Something had gone wrong during Jill's labor and by the time the doctor could get to the babies it was too late. Their tiny hearts had stopped beating. There was nothing more they could do. Jill was alive but emotionally devastated.

When I hung up the phone, I was sick. All I could think about was how I needed to do *something*. *What was it I was supposed to do?*

The earlier urging was gone, but it had been replaced by a compelling feeling of responsibility. I hadn't done anything to help prevent this tragedy, but now I knew I had to do *something*. I just didn't yet know what.

The next day, for lack of a better idea, I went to my mom's, where she and I, along with my grandmother, cooked food all day. Jill was being discharged from the hospital and after she and her husband made funeral arrangements they would be walking into a lonely house with two empty baby beds in a newly decorated nursery. We knew no one would be in any condition to cook and, with her two children from her first marriage and her in-laws from a nearby state joining them there that evening, it seemed bringing food was the best thing we could do.

I'd been spared hearing that horrid question when suddenly, as I was standing in my mom's kitchen mashing potatoes, it returned: "What are you going to do for Jill?"

I shuddered at the thought of it, for it was just that—a thought—but it was definitely originating from someplace not of my own creation and was directed specifically at me. Although I was beginning to understand from Whom it was emanating, I fell back into my old pattern of arguing with Him.

"I'm fixing food for Jill! What more do I have to do?" I was growing angry about the entire situation. "Tell me what to do! If you want me to do something, tell me what you want me to do!" I tried to keep my back turned from my mom and grandmother and pretend to be completely engrossed in my mashed potato duties.

When I started across the kitchen to retrieve the milk from the refrigerator, what I heard literally stopped me in my tracks.

"You need to sing a song for Jill."

I almost dropped the milk as I returned to my workstation and tried to hide my shock.

"What do you mean, I need to sing a song for Jill? I *can't* sing a song for her!"

He persisted: "You need to sing a song for Jill."

"I can't sing! With the exception of that brief practice last night, I haven't sung in front of anyone in years. I don't even know a complete song from start to finish, much less one that would be appropriate for Jill in this situation. I can't do it."

"You need to sing a song for Jill."

I was growing frantic.

"It's going to be cold and raining, and I'm going to be too upset to sing. I've only sung at one funeral in my life. It was nearly impossible, and it wasn't even a family member's funeral. And even if I did know a song and I did think I could get through it, I wouldn't have any accompaniment or back-up, and I've never sung a solo under any circumstance. It's simply not possible."

"You need to sing a song for Jill."

I was exasperated.

"Okay," I resigned, "when I take this food to Jill, if she specifically asks me to sing a particular song, then I will sing it. Otherwise, there's nothing I can do." I thought I had finally reached an acceptable compromise, and just in the nick of time, because we were about to load up and drive to Jill's.

It was such an indescribably sad scene. They really appreciated what we had done, but no one really knew what to do or say. We helplessly muttered, "I'm so sorry," then sat quietly waiting for Jill to speak. She showed us photos of her two perfect and beautiful little girls all cleaned up and dressed in pink shortly after their untimely death. We all cried and hugged and waited—waited for the right thing to say, waited for some indication this was going to work out alright, and waited for some sign that God had not abandoned us during this tragic time.

I personally waited for Jill to ask me to sing. She didn't ask. I didn't bring it up. After all, I didn't want to seem pushy. And the previously nagging message, this time, was silent. I drove away from Jill's house thinking I had done all that could or should be expected of me under these circumstances.

With the private graveside service planned for the following morning, I'd decided to spend the night with my grandmother in order to rise early and help her get to the cemetery on time. We sat around for a few minutes after returning from Jill's and very quickly the conversation headed in that dreaded direction.

"What do you think we should do for Jill?" Granny asked me. I almost groaned out loud.

"I don't know what else to do for her, Granny," I whined, wondering how many different sources of this urging I would have to face. I convinced Granny I was too tired to think about it and with obvious reluctance she retired to her bedroom.

When I lay down, although I felt exhausted, sleep would not come. My mind was racing, as I mentally reviewed every second of the last two days. Then Granny came tottering to my door.

"Maybe we should disassemble the baby beds," she offered.

"Yes, maybe we should," I replied.

After she vetted that idea aloud for a few moments, she wandered back to bed, only to return just minutes later.

"Maybe we should purchase plastic totes and pack up all the baby clothes and supplies," she now offered.

"I guess we could stop and get some totes on the way to the cemetery," I replied, desperately wanting this to be her last little visit.

I don't know why she bothered to go back to bed. It seemed like I blinked my eyes and she was back.

"Maybe we should stop somewhere after the funeral and purchase lunch to take back to Jill's house."

"Maybe we should do all three." I would have agreed with anything at this point. Were we never going to rest?

I listened for the scuffing of Granny's unsure steps to wander across the hall again but heard none. So I closed my eyes and tried to will myself to sleep. As I lay there suspended between wakefulness and sleep, once again I heard the now-familiar urging in my head.

"You need to sing a song for Jill."

"Oh, please," I begged for mercy, "Jill didn't ask me to sing, and I don't know a song to sing for her."

Then, as if on cue—as if someone had turned on a radio—a melody began to waft through my head. What was it? I'd heard it before. Yes, that was it. It was, "Lamb of God," one of the five new songs I'd practiced for the first time the night before with The Joyful Noises group. It played over and over again like a stuck record.

"Okay, so what if I remember the tune?" I pleaded. "How can I sing this song for Jill? I don't remember the words."

Then again, clearly on cue this time, I began to hear the words. It was a short song—three verses and a chorus.

Wait! Three verses? There were only two verses. I was sure of it. When we'd practiced it the previous evening, the sopranos had sung the first verse and the tenors sang the second. I actually should not have even remembered more than the sopranos' verse. But as the song droned on through my consciousness, I clearly heard it again— the two original verses and chorus—and a new third verse. Cold chills ran down my body as I swung my feet to the floor. All my resistance melted away. Bursting into Granny's bedroom, I exclaimed, "Granny, I need some paper and something to write with!"

You know, I've learned a lot from my Granny over the years, but I learned something unexpected during those twelve hours at her house. When you're in your seventies there are two things you don't own—an alarm clock that works (we had to ask my parents for a *wake-up call)* and paper. I guess you just don't have much use for either at that age.

Surprisingly, without requesting any explanation, Granny began to scurry about searching for something. In my sleepy stupor, I tried to commit the words of the song to memory while she, with great haste, dug and hunted and finally returned with all she could find—a short, dull pencil and a small pocket calendar, which was about ten years out of date. It had the days of the month listed three per page and a small space for notes. I accepted it and feverishly wrote the *three* verses and the chorus. Surprisingly, Granny still didn't ask about my unusual behavior. It was as if she already knew.

I finished my task and thanked her. We said goodnight again and returned to our beds. Before I turned out the light, I looked at the clock on the wall. It read eleven-thirty. This time, when I laid my head down on the pillow, Granny didn't show up at my door and the music in my head had stopped. I was at peace and went right to sleep.

The next morning, rested and refreshed, reason began to creep back in. Who was I kidding? I couldn't go through with this. But now Granny had seen me writing it down and although she hadn't asked, she had to suspect it. So as we sat waiting for my parents to pick us up, I sheepishly confessed to her that I was thinking about singing a song at the funeral.

With what had become in the last twelve hours an unusual disregard for caution, Granny quickly blurted out, "I think you should do it!" She didn't even ask me about the song itself.

"I'm afraid I can't get through it," I admitted.

"Just don't look at anyone and sing it," She persisted,

Now the cat was out of the bag and I knew Granny would try to hold me to it. I tried to muster my courage on the ride to the cemetery. But when I saw Jill—humped over in her chair in front of the tiny blue casket that contained both babies, surrounded by her husband and two children, all so distraught and heartbroken—my courage melted away. I was ready to give up when I heard the urging.

"Sing that song for Jill!"

Somehow I knew I would never forgive myself if I didn't heed this instruction. My adrenaline started pumping. I had only a few minutes to decide. I swallowed hard, snuck up behind Jill, leaned forward, whispered in her ear, and asked if she wanted someone to sing. She looked up with tear-filled eyes and said, "If you want to."

I rushed over to the pastor, who was ready to begin, and told him I was going to sing.

"Do you want to do it at the beginning or at the end?" he asked.

"The end," I said, acting as if I knew what I was doing.

"Before or after the prayer?"

"Before."

He nodded, and I walked back over and took my place underneath the funeral home tent, standing behind the two rows of chairs beside Granny. I could feel myself trembling. And when Jill's young children began to cry, soon there was not a dry eye in the place. I wanted to run back to the pastor and tell him to let me sing first. I just knew I wouldn't be able to sing after I had stood there and had cried through the service. But, it was too late. He was already beginning.

When the pastor began to speak, I felt a growing lump in my throat. The link between what he was saying and the words of the song I had been given to sing, especially the new last verse, startled me. The realization washed over me that not only was I meant to sing for Jill, but also I was meant to sing this very song—the specific new verse. Having learned the song only hours before hearing the babies had died, I realized I'd been led the entire time, from the first moment I felt compelled to do something for Jill, to go to the new church, to sing with The Joyful Noises. I had not waited until it was too late after all. *This was what I was supposed to do for Jill.*

It must have been this realization that enabled me, when the pastor gave me the nod, to swallow the lump in my throat, take a long deep breath, and begin to sing. Clutching the crumpled pages from Granny's calendar in my trembling hands, I sang those three verses as earnestly as I could through the tears that streamed down my face, knowing they were God's message of comfort for Jill, especially the new verse:

> Your plan for me, I could not see
> Though you were walking beside me.
> Draw near me now, and lead me home.
> Help me walk on, sweet Lamb of God.

The pastor, noticeably moved by the strong tie between the messages God had used the two of us to deliver, gave the closing benediction, and everyone began milling around and moving slowly toward their cars.

I looked up to see Jill walking toward me with the first smile I'd seen on her face all morning.

"Rhonda," she spoke softly, "When you brought the food to my house last night, I wanted to ask you if you would sing, but I was afraid that would be asking too much of you."

I felt the tears stinging my eyes. I wanted to say, "That's okay, Jill. Trust me, you didn't have to ask. It was already taken care of." Instead I just smiled back.

She continued, "Do you think I could have the words to that song?"

I chuckled as I looked down at the calendar pages still crumpled in my hand.

"I'll need to type them for you."

"Well, you can send them to me. I would just like to have a copy of it, because it was so comforting. Everything the pastor said in his message and the words of your song just tied in perfectly with what we've been feeling since last night. Thank you so much for singing that song. It was so peaceful."

She went on to tell me how she and her husband couldn't sleep the night before, so they had stayed up talking.

"And, you know," she said, "we were trying to understand what had happened and why, and we were so distraught. Then all of a sudden we were just overcome with a wonderful feeling of peace. We realized that we wouldn't know in this lifetime the answers to why our babies had to go so soon. But we do know we will see them again in heaven, and we will all be together forever. Once we realized that, we just relaxed and went to sleep."

I was fighting back the emotions. "Jill, what time was it that you finally got to sleep?"

"It was eleven-thirty," she replied, "I remember because I had to set the alarm."

I smiled at Jill. It was the same time at which I'd finally relented and followed God's guidance.

I've thought about that sequence of events over and over again since that day now over a decade ago. I don't claim to understand why those two beautiful baby girls, Hannah Grace and Sarah Elise, didn't make it into this world to know how much we all loved them. I find comfort, nonetheless, in knowing that God was at work among us. Not just during the last days of the ordeal, but right from the beginning. For reasons we cannot comprehend, He knew what was going to happen, and He was preparing all the while to not only minister to Jill's broken spirit but also to teach me what it means to have faith in Him.

Amazing Faith—that's the title of this collection of writings. But I surely don't claim to possess an amazing faith. No, as you can clearly see, if anything, I possess a hesitant, sometimes faltering faith. But what this experience and others has taught me is that if I will only act, even upon faith as tiny as a mustard seed, when that faith is placed in an awesome God, it can yield amazing results.

With this experience, God taught me it wasn't about me—not how I looked or sounded or how well I performed. I cried and choked up—

my voice trembling and breaking—throughout the song. Still God used that to minister to Jill in her time of need. It was God's words for Jill being delivered through me. Had I not been faithful to respond to God's call, Jill would not have received that comfort, and I would not have learned this profound lesson.

Sometimes God calls us to demonstrate our faith, because He needs to minister to others through us. Sometimes He calls us to act upon our faith, so He can teach us an important lesson. Sometimes He calls us to faithfully step outside our comfort zone for both purposes at once. The key, common to any and every case, is to act.

I saw a message on a church sign recently that said, "Faith is believing in things not seen." This is true, but I've learned faith is more than just believing. If I say I believe in something, but you never see me do anything to prove it, wouldn't you doubt whether I truly believed it? Faith is *acting* upon what we say we believe. Belief is a starting point. Good intentions are fine; but true faith is our belief and good intentions in action. The beauty is, when demonstrated, faith benefits you and all those around you.

If you're struggling in your belief . . . just act. In the same way God revealed His love and omnipresence to me through this situation with Jill, He will reveal Himself to you when you act for Him. And in this way, He will strengthen your belief and grow your faith.

"For the Lord is good and His love endures forever; His faithfulness continues through all generations"—Psalm 100:5.

May you find your courage today to act in Christ Jesus so that you may experience His great blessings, even in the midst of your darkest days.

RHONDA JONES is a master storyteller, most well known for the true stories woven from her country roots and the important lessons she learned living and worshiping in the tight-knit, faithful community of her childhood. She leads readers and listeners alike on humor-filled, heartwarming, and insightful journeys that transform the ordinary into extraordinary. She has served as Director of Ministry Programs at Living Water Church and is the owner of Bright Hope Training & Consulting. She is the author of *Teaching Common Sense: Seven Simple Principles for Nurturing Those Around You* and *Reaping the Harvest of Your Life.*

Rhonda Jones
Bright Hope Consulting
P.O. Box 50730
Knoxville, Tennessee 37950
Phone / Fax: 865.769.7510
E-mail: Rhonda@BrightHopeConsulting.com
www.brighthopeconsulting.com
www.rhondajones.us

Barbara Parentini

At The Speed of Love

This story is dedicated to my Heavenly Father
whose immovable loving presence carried me
from the valley to the mountaintop.

"He delivers and rescues, and He works signs and
wonders in heaven and on earth"—Daniel 6:27 (NKJV).

It was a perfect summer night. A golden full moon was climbing
behind the towering pines, bathing the sky in moonlight. As I
turned the car toward home, fragrant gusts of honeysuckle and
freshly mowed grass poured in the open windows, tossing my hair in
every direction. Childhood memories emerged of night rides in Dad's
old, black Ford with the top down, listening to "Little Jimmy Brown"
on the radio. We'd cruise into the Frostop Drive-In to eat foot-long
coneys and drink root beer floats under the stars. . . Life was simpler
then. A red traffic light pulled me into the present, fading the care-
free images like movie credits on a dark screen.

Turning into the village, I eased the car onto the grassy shoulder
and turned off the motor. The June night was still except for the soft
sound of crickets in the pasture and flickers of fireflies. Never had I
seen a more breathtaking sky. It was here in these lush gardens with
bluebirds and wildlife that God had granted the desires of my nature-
loving heart.

"You are an awesome God," I whispered in the darkness. Grateful
for the gift of life, I shuddered to think how close I had come to losing

mine. As the moon turned cool silver in the night sky, my thoughts revisited autumn two and a half years ago. . . .

In mid-September 2003, my husband, Brian, and I were excited to move to a pastoral village in North Carolina. After a stressful year, we gladly traded the suburbs for grazing cows and gracious English gardens. Autumn was already casting a golden light under canopies of red and yellow leaves, and we were eager to settle in for my folks' visit three weeks away.

During their brief visit, they encouraged me to join them in late October for Mom's seventieth birthday celebration. Plans to decorate the house and enrollment forms for UNC would have to wait. Two days later at the airport, I waved goodbye to Brian and flew to sunny Florida. Little did I know that my feet would not touch the velvet sands of Siesta Key, and my life was about to change forever.

Once at my folks' home in Sarasota, I was spellbound by God's handiwork. White pelicans glided like swans on the blue-green sea, and dolphins could be sighted playing in the sparkling bay. In the evening, sunsets burned crimson and orange into nights cooled by salty sea breezes. It was destined to be two weeks of fun and relaxation.

A few days later, as I drove Dad to visit his friend, John, who was in a nursing home, he told me how John had hit his head during an episode of seizures, causing serious brain damage. For days, maybe weeks, John's life hung in the balance. Dad and other church members prayed and faithfully visited him each week. He'd regained consciousness, but had a long way to go to make a full recovery. That afternoon before leaving, Dad chose a passage for me to read from the book of Psalms, and slid his large-print Bible across the table. We closed with prayer for his friend's continued healing and headed for home.

Later that evening, while the family gathered at an outdoor restaurant on the beach, we planned another visit for the next afternoon. I was happy to be part of Dad's weekly visitations, and to spend precious time with him. He had studied the Bible since his conversion in his twenties and often shared personal, exciting stories of his walk with the Lord. The gentleman we were to visit, known as Brother Allen, had been sent to hospice the year before with end-stage kidney disease and a myriad of serious illnesses. To everyone's amazement, he actually got better and was "kicked out" after several months! Dad chuckled as he recounted the nurse saying to Allen one morning, "If you're not going to die, you're going to have to go home!" He was certain all the earnest prayers of his friends had made a difference in his outcome.

The next morning I awakened to an azure sky and swam laps after breakfast. Moving through the turquoise water, I watched seagulls dart and glide over the lanai, and lifted the Psalm, "This is the day the Lord has made. We will rejoice and be glad in it" (Psalm 118:24 NKJV). Later that afternoon we climbed into the shiny blue pick-up, and like the day before, Dad placed his large-print Bible on the dashboard and buckled up. I chose not to. I'd rationalized for years that seatbelts aggravated the scoliosis in my back and made me miserable. Before leaving the driveway, back discomfort sent me running into the garage for two beach towels to sit on. As we pulled away, the sparkling indigo of the bay disappeared in the rearview mirror, leaving no indication that I wouldn't be home for sunset, not tonight—not for weeks to come.

The Friday afternoon rush was already visible as we traveled toward Bradenton on Route 41, a six-lane highway notorious for its danger and heavy traffic. Minutes down the road at a congested intersection, we navigated a right turn, and the bumper-to-bumper traffic gleamed in the afternoon sun like a giant caterpillar. Moving cautiously, I spotted up ahead the nose of a car poised to make a beeline across several lanes of traffic. It was an illegal maneuver, but reckless drivers were seen everywhere on these roads. I made a mental note of the car and within moments, we merged with the flow of traffic.

Suddenly a streak of white flashed in my peripheral vision. Stunned, I watched a white car accelerate toward my door. I yelled a warning to Dad, "He's going to hit us!" In an instant, the intruder gunned it and crashed into us broadside. The impact of metal and glass was deafening. The violent movement of the truck sent us reeling across the front of the car and I gripped the steering wheel that spun uncontrollably to the right as the truck began to flip. In an instant, I lunged forward hitting my head and then I lost consciousness. According to Dad, after we completely flipped over and landed upright, my seat was empty and he saw me lying on the road.

The events that followed were like vivid snapshots—timeless and profound. Totally blinded, I heard a very loud sound like the sound in a high-velocity wind tunnel. Engulfed in the sound I felt I was moving very fast. I distinctly remember having a sense of regret about Brian. We'd only been married six years. I questioned, "Am I on my way to heaven?" There was a point of awareness deep within, even in unconsciousness . . . no fear, no sounds of traffic or glass breaking, simply peace.

I awakened on the scorching asphalt surrounded by strangers kneeling, urging me not to move. Someone returned with towels from the truck to slide under my leg searing on the pavement. Before slipping into unconsciousness, I looked up to see the unforgettable expression of pain and fright in Dad's eyes as he pleaded, "Barbie, Barbie." My critical hour was counting down as the helicopter soared above the coastal waters to the trauma center. In the ambulance, Dad continued to ask, "Is my daughter going to be all right?" Thankfully, except for a few minor cuts and sore ribs, he was not seriously hurt and returned home that evening.

Mom was alone in the house when the phone rang with the awful news of the ambulance rushing us to the hospital and moments later the dreaded update of my airlift to another city. Her hands shook as she dialed the number for her sister, Aunt Joy, who reassured Mom she was on her way. The prayers of loved ones, friends, and clergy took flight. Two or more were gathering. Two aunts in Kentucky paused in a parking lot to pray, six churches were alerted to pray, and the chaplain summoned Brian with grave news to come right away. A taproot of faith was pulsing with prayers of believers, and our lives were being lifted up on the powerful arms of the Holy Spirit.

Life below went on according to plan. People rushed home to their families and friends for Friday night pizza and lovers strolled along the gentle surf. But God had a different plan. He would not allow the enemy to destroy my life. At the intersection of life and death, God rescued me and propelled me toward my destiny in Him *at the speed of love.*

The hours that followed were blurred and punctuated by pain and shock. Near nine in the evening, I was jarred by the commanding voice of a nurse in the trauma room giving a report about a patient with multiple fractures of the pelvis, tibia, fibula, humerus, lumbar, and sacral something, lacerated spleen . . . her voice trailed off. Thank God, no one mentioned the airstrip from my bangs to the crown of my head that sheared my hair like a burr. Alarmed, I thought she couldn't be talking about me. She was.

That first night on the trauma unit was like a strange dream. Pain medication clouded my thinking and fine black lines chased my eye movements like water spiders skating on creek water. I tried to pray, but thoughts were too slippery to hold. Anxious and broken, I called out for strength and healing. *My faith was being tested on a whole new level.* I started and restarted the twenty-third Psalm. Over and over I coaxed the words from my memory, "The Lord is my shepherd I shall not want" . . . the words escaped . . . "The Lord is my shepherd, I shall not want, He makes me to lie down in green pastures . . . " I held on to each line for dear life. Like a lamb with a broken leg, the Good Shepherd gently carried me through the valley of the shadow of death and eased my fear in my darkest hour. His mercy granted me rest in green pastures, and still living waters refreshed my thirsty spirit as I drifted off to sleep, blanketed in the promises of Psalm 23. While nurses scurried to their patients' bedsides and a helicopter roared in and out above the room all night to rescue the injured, I was being transformed by the loving presence of Jesus.

Joy surged when Brian arrived early in the morning. Fatigued from driving all night, his tired eyes glistened with tears.

"Honey? Honey, are you all right?" he asked softly. He cradled my bruised hand, and leaned down to kiss my cheek. I nodded yes as he searched my eyes to see if I was telling the truth. His expression was one of sweet gratitude, as if I were the Homecoming Queen and he was the lucky guy taking me to the dance. Not once did his expression betray the train-wreck of a wife he saw. All week he barely left my side except to shower and sleep. Brian would make seven trips to Florida before flying me home in January. His tenderness and devotion anchored our marriage, and our love for each other shone like a beacon in the dark.

The next evening, anxious family members and relatives gathered in the trauma room. With apologetic smiles they expressed their disbelief, while others quietly dabbed tears. Their presence brought such comfort and encouragement. Questions sparked about the accident and I shared my experience about the loud wind. I just needed to talk about it . . . and I did—to anyone who would listen.

Aunt Becky asked me in her southern drawl, "Was it like a 'mighty rushing wind'?"

My eyes scanned the room, "What was that?"

Again she asked, "Like a 'mighty rushing wind'?"

My ears perked, "That's what it was all right." A few nervous chuckles rippled through the group.

Becky smiled, "Barb, that's the Holy Spirit!"

"It is?" I asked.

"Yes, read Acts 2:2."

I believed her affirmation. God was present to protect us, and that mighty wind had ushered in new life for me.

Late that night the horror of what happened began to sink in. I talked to God about the significance of this life-changing experience. In the silence the Holy Spirit whispered, "Life is a gift. Life is a gift." He urged me to service, not to wait. From that moment I was stirred with an urgency to share God's message of love and grace with others.

After a week on the trauma unit, a stretcher wheeled me down a shiny, checkerboard corridor to a special rehab floor. I had agreed to work very hard in physical therapy. Aside from morning and afternoon sessions six days a week and one session on Sunday, I was on bedrest. I wrestled with pain and exhaustion, but gradually adapted to the uphill climb of rehab. The visits of family and relatives, bundles of encouraging cards, and beautiful flowers made the long days bearable. There were many believers there, including my roommate, Jean, whose special gift was encouragement. Late in the evening we'd pray out loud, softly sing our favorite hymns, and share stories about our lives. We especially loved it when Ella, a petite nurse on fire for Jesus, would boldly deliver her prayers over us. She'd grip my hands with the strength of an usher greeting visitors on Sunday morning. In a Martin Luther King style, she'd speak her prayers with a fearless determination, and always closed by saying, "In the mighty name of Jesus." I loved her.

After a month, near Thanksgiving, I was discharged to my folks' home in Sarasota to recuperate. Absorbed in the tranquil beauty of the bay from the hospital bed, there was time as I'd never known before—time to rest, time to be still and wait in the Lord's presence, and time to delight in His goodness. There was time to be entertained by my sweet nieces and enjoy conversations with Mom about the good old days. Aunt Joy pampered me by shaving my legs in bed and bringing wonderful music CDs and decadent desserts.

There was also precious time sitting with Dad in his cozy paneled den to discuss scripture, to pray, or to listen to *Nocturne,* a bedtime radio broadcast with Bill Caldwell. Some evenings he'd tune in to Erwin Lutzer from Moody Church in Chicago, or the late Zola Levitt, a Messianic Jew who passionately shared the Gospel around the globe. And I'd be wiping tears when Billy Graham gave the altar call to "Just As I Am" on *Crusade Classics.* Each night on his way to bed, Dad sat at my bedside and spoke prayers of blessings and healing on my life.

Those were special days with family. Three years later, a gift book would dawn with nuggets of gold from those memories, *In the Den with Daniel: Lessons Dad Taught Me about Our Heavenly Father.*

I'd only begun to realize the changes that I'd undergone. From the moment I opened my eyes in the hospital, I knew I was changed. Not only did I feel different in my body, I felt different emotionally, as if the awe and wonder of childhood had been miraculously restored. The changes also seemed to afford me a discernment of people and situations with more clarity than ever before. I embraced others with more love and many people remarked, "You sure have a positive attitude for what you've been through." The greatest change was the sense of urgency ignited to share the message of God's unconditional love and grace with others.

It would be months before focusing on a page or steady concentration returned well enough to write my testimony, but days before Christmas the words to a poem flowed about Jesus appearing in a dream. This poem was to become the first Christmas card printed for Gifts by Grace.

I was waiting on the Lord and He was renewing my strength on many levels. He faithfully lifted me on wings like eagles over the painful road of recovery. God used the quiet hours in His Word to prepare me for the race ahead. I trusted Him to make it to the finish line and my faith was growing.

On a windy January night, Brian and I flew home to North Carolina. Anticipation mounted as we drove past small trees draped with white lights in our village and we saw deer skirting into the dark woods.

Within days our lives revolved around endless sessions of pool therapy, physical therapy appointments, and doctor visits. Brian had become a skilled caregiver and took pride in meeting my needs. While I completed routines in the warm water pool, he used the time to walk the track on the floor above. When we'd catch a glimpse of each other, we'd wave and smile. Brian had been true to his marriage vows. Our love for each other was deeper now than ever and we joked that we were "joined at the hip."

In the spring of 2004, the church invited me to share my transformation story on Pentecost Sunday. Writing was a struggle the first few days, and I wrestled with self-doubt. The enemy was depending on my unfinished English degree, interrupted by the accident eighteen months prior to graduation, to discourage any hopes of serious writing. The Holy Spirit stilled my protests of self-reliance. He revealed that writing was more than a rewarding ability, it was a calling for which He would inspire and equip me. Soon after I dedicated all my talents to God, words flowed from my pen onto the paper.

One summer night, I Googled the Web for Christian writers and landed on Jerry Jenkins' Christian Writers Guild Web site. I was excited to read that the Conference, with its host of authors and editors, was coming up at The Cove, Billy Graham's Training Center in Asheville. I joined and registered that night. Brian was not available to drive me five hours across the state, so I prayed that my confidence behind the wheel would equal my longing to attend.

The day I left, excitement overshadowed any physical discomfort. After reaching Statesville, only two and a half hours from home, I stopped for the night. The next afternoon, driving deeper into the Blue Ridge Mountains, I was unprepared for the splendor I was about to witness. From the moment I was greeted at the gate and drove up the steep road that wound along lush flowerbeds and pine-scented woods to the lodge, a peace settled over me so profound that tears flowed down my cheeks. The peaceful presence that embraced the mountain never lifted that week.

A spirit of service emanated from the faces of the extraordinary staff. While they unpacked my car, I approached the dormitory reception desk, steadied on two canes. There on the wall directly in front of me, carved in a large piece of warm wood, was the twenty-third Psalm. Like a powerful sign, those comforting promises I'd clung to in the trauma unit were now affirming my obedience to a divine call. The words leapt off the beautiful carving and I remembered Dad's remarks in his den, "God's word is alive!" Overwhelmed with emotion, I sank into a nearby chair and quietly wept tears of joy.

Bright and early the next morning, I joined a group of authors and aspiring Christian writers for our first class on gift books and devotionals taught by Vicki Caruana. A schoolteacher by profession, Vicki had authored the devotional series *Apples and Chalkdust*, a favorite among educators. Her ability to distill years of hard-earned experience in the world of publishing prepared us to submit a proposal by the week's end. We learned volumes and left inspired about crafting our own gift books and devotionals from this talented Christian writer.

In between meetings, I pushed my wheelchair filled with belongings through the spacious lodge. Walls of glass met expanses of stone and rich mahogany moldings. A reverential hush filled the long hallways lined with photography, paintings, and display cases that depicted Dr. Billy Graham's life as an evangelist. The powerful photos captured his many friends throughout the world, his beloved wife, Ruth, his family, and crusades over the decades. The Cove, a living tribute to Billy Graham's global outreach, bore witness to a life lived fully for Christ.

One evening while standing alone in a shadowy corridor waiting for the evening program to conclude, Gloria Gaither walked over to me. She glanced at my canes and asked softly what had happened to me. After I shared a little about the accident, she replied in her gentle manner, "You were broken, now God can use you." She went on to say it was going to be interesting to see how God would be working in my life in the days ahead.

On the last day of the Conference, I said goodbyes to new friends and walked onto the huge deck overlooking spectacular blue vistas. I was on the mountaintop. I'd come by faith, not by sight, as God beckoned to trust Him. I'd caught a glimpse of divine possibilities, a plan that promised hope, and a future filled with His purpose for my life. With a grateful heart, I came down from the mountain rejoicing.

Walking by faith did not translate into a pain-free life. Though I was fortunate not to suffer from a full-blown post-traumatic stress syndrome (a treacherous response to trauma that can last for years), the horror of the accident had stripped my nervous system, leaving me as emotionally vulnerable as an exposed nerve. There were disappointments along the way. Loved ones and friends I longed to see, failed to call or visit, and uncaring comments by others inflicted its own brand of wounding. God's Word ministered comfort to me through Romans, "The insults of those who insult you have fallen on me" (Romans 15:3 NIV). Sensitive by nature, I plumbed new depths of suffering, not only my own, but with a deeper compassion for the pain of others.

During the long months of immobility and solitude, I found blessings in simple things. Slender dogwood branches veiled with creamy porcelain blossoms, a songbird's melody, or vibrant ruby-red geraniums on the deck touched my heart with their beauty.

Hobbies shelved for years were rekindled into hours of fun with my nieces—painting on rainy afternoons, sewing specialty pillows, and decorating tall cakes with butter cream wedding cake frosting. None of my suffering and abilities was wasted. As I created cards and wrote thoughtful inscriptions, God breathed new inspiration into my passion for words and desire to create something beautiful. I'd often awaken at four in the morning flooded with ideas as the Holy Spirit flowed like Teletype from my pen.

In the spring of 2005, Gifts by Grace was born. Soaring Hearts Cards and a budding gift line spoke hope, encouragement, and love to the receiver. Faithful to His word in Psalm 37:4, "Delight yourself in the Lord and He will give you the desires of your heart," He granted some desires and erased others not aligned with His will. Once again, boundless grace transformed the most despairing circumstances into something beautiful.

A year after attending the Christian Writers Guild Conference, I followed Vicki Caruana's advice and traveled to a C.L.A.S.S. (Christian Leaders, Authors, Speakers Services) seminar in Knoxville, Tennessee. Having listened to numerous C.L.A.S.S. CDs prior to the seminar, I was thrilled to finally meet the veteran authors and speakers, Florence Littauer and her daughter, Maurita Littauer. The Conference was teeming with staff and participants who'd come from around the globe. Each day, Florence and Maurita brought down the house with wonderful spirit-led presentations and C.L.A.S.S. staff members contributed a wealth of information from their speaking and writing ministries.

Florence's outgoing personality and polished style reflected a lovely outward appearance, yet it was her caring spirit that radiated a deeply committed servant's heart. We all felt privileged to sit under her tutelage that week.

As I took inventory at C.L.A.S.S., one thing was clear: I was in need of an extreme makeover! The accident had devastated my self-image and concerns about physical appearance had been pushed to the back burner. I confess I was just so glad to be alive that I really didn't care much about my appearance. The reality was I walked like someone thirty years my senior, my ears rang like a chorus of crickets, and I'd developed a glowing rosacea aggravated by months in the ninety-four-degree physical therapy pool. And though my hair had always been my best asset, it had fallen out by the handfuls. A slate color was taking over the back and a silvery fringe across the top and sides—I resembled a skunk!

Eleven months after the accident, my hairdresser snipped off the last trace of auburn hair and a new image emerged. Women often stopped me to offer a compliment about my hair and asked what I did to get the lovely color effects. I was surprised by their response. In time, a close friend confided that even my countenance had changed.

After all, how was it that I could be flipped several times with glass everywhere, thrown to the highway, suffer trauma and injuries that often result in paralysis or death, and not have my skull fractured, facial bones broken, teeth knocked out, or lose limbs? Mysteriously, my spleen stopped bleeding days later, and none of my fractures required casts or surgery. In fact, after a lifetime of back discomfort, I no longer suffer with lumbar back pain from the scoliosis and my posture is straighter. Surely, "By His stripes I was healed" (Isaiah 53:5 NIV).

This sacred journey of faith was one of adventure, risk, and discovery. The Lord called me to trust Him and Him alone—more than my doctors, more than my education, and more than my self-designed identity. The Holy Spirit illuminated areas of my life not fully yielded to Jesus. He also gave insight into the lives of people around me who were sacrificing their health and relationships on the altar of work, ambition, or addiction only to realize that when life came crashing down around them, self could not fill their emptiness and longing. I saw that people everywhere were hungry for God and to know that He loved them beyond anything they ever imagined. Jesus continued to teach me that faith meant stepping out in trust to follow Him into deep water—that discipleship was risky business. I trusted Him and His redeeming grace was making my broken vessel whole.

Sounds in a distant pasture broke the silence. There in the sky, a wide corona of light encircled the moon, soft rainbows shimmering in its gossamer swath. Like a divine smile, I could feel the pleasure of the Father and thanked Him for the gift of life. I memorized one last look and the holy moment filled me with unspeakable joy. I started the car and inched through the passageway of trees, their white lights twinkling like Christmas. I wanted to pinch myself to see if I was dreaming, but this was no dream. This was the overflow—the abundant stuff, like juicy watermelon that runs down your arm and drips off your elbow.

Moonlight swept ribbons of silver across the black water as I drove past the pond. I recalled a conversation that Dad told me he'd had with the state trooper at the scene of the accident:

She had said, "I hope you know how lucky you are that your daughter is alive. Seventy percent of people thrown from vehicles are killed, but after I looked in your truck, I knew why you and your daughter weren't."

"Why is that?" he asked.

She motioned, "That book on your dashboard."

Dad went over to take a look. Miraculously, there on the dashboard was his Bible.

In his words, "It never moved."

Isn't it just like God to show up with His unchanging, immovable love in the intersections of life? It wasn't my faith that was so amazing—it was His miraculous, redeeming, amazing grace that made all the difference. Celebrate life!

Acknowledgments:

I am deeply grateful to the following: My parents, Daniel and Loretta Green, who nurtured my love for God, nature's splendor, and passion for the arts; for Dad's affection and belief in me, and Mom's inspiration to attend a Christian Writers Guild Conference; my sister, Danielle, and my nieces, Hadley and Anna, for their laughter and love; Kathleen, my mother-in-law, for her helpful spirit; relatives and friends who prayed, assisted in my care, brought cheer with their visits, fed us like royalty; for cards of encouragement and surrounding my family with loving support.

Ella, Bayfront Trauma Center and Bayflite's lifesaving staff was a Godsend. The pastors and churches that prayed and encouraged me during the crisis and recovery.

Laurel, Aunt Joy, Leava, Marge, Chris, Maggie, Elizabeth, Carolyn, Pat, Rita, Donna, Carol, and Gail, for friendship worth its weight in gold.

And to Brian, my sweet husband, for the patience of a saint. Your love is my treasure.

BARBARA PARENTINI, a native Ohioan, fell in love with the South when she attended Warren Wilson College in the Blue Ridge Mountains. Retired from her career as a registered nurse since a car accident in 2003, she devotes much of her time writing Christian devotional books, creative non-fiction, and fiction. Her recent contributions appear in *One Year Life Verse* by Jay K. Payleitner, published by Tyndale House, October 2007, and *Good Morning Christian Writer Devotional* by Crystal A. Murray, due out in 2008.

She enjoys creating her card line Soaring Hearts; also, *Living Letters: Letters from the Heart, Letters that Heal,* a retreat and journal available in 2008. Barbara is a graduate of C.L.A.S.S. She and her husband, Brian, reside near Chapel Hill, North Carolina.

Barbara Parentini
Gifts by Grace
E-mail: barbara@barbaraparentini.com
www.barbaraparentini.com
(Photo credit: Missy McLamb Photographers)

Dr. Robert Schuller

A Special Interview

David E. Wright (Wright)

Robert Harold Schuller was born in Alton, Iowa. He was raised on his parents' farm nearby, in a small, close-knit community of Dutch Americans. Robert knew from the early age of four that he wanted to be a minister of the church. After graduating from a tiny high school of nearby Newkirk, Iowa, he entered Hope College in Holland, Michigan, where he earned a Bachelor of Arts degree. Robert was ready to return to Michigan to pursue his religious studies at Western Theological Seminary. In 1950, he received his Master of Divinity degree. The young Reverend Schuller married Arvella DeHann of Newkirk, and the newlyweds moved to Chicago where the newly ordained minister took up his first assignment as pastor of the Ivanhoe Reformed Church. During his ministry, the congregation grew from thirty-eight to over four hundred. In 1955, Schuller's denomination, the Reformed Church of America, called on him to build a new congregation in Garden Grove, California. With only $500 in assets, he decided to rent a drive-in movie theater, the Orange Drive-in. On the first Sunday, one hundred persons attended services seated in their cars, while Reverend Schuller preached from the tarpaper roof of the snack bar. The Garden Grove congregation continued to grow. When a larger building was needed, Rev. Schuller commissioned the renowned architect Phillip Johnson to build a new building, all of glass. It would come to be known as the Crystal Cathedral. After almost insurmountable difficulties, this 2,736-seat architectural marvel was dedicated in 1980,

"To the Glory of Man for the Greater Glory of God." Today, one million people visit the Cathedral annually. Dr. Schuller is the author of over thirty books, six of which have found a place on the *New York Times* and *Publisher's Weekly* bestseller lists.

Dr. Schuller, welcome to *Amazing Faith.*

Dr. Robert Schuller (Schuller)
Thank you, David.

Wright
Dr. Schuller, you have stated, "I learn from my dad to dream, even when the dream seems impossible." Would you tell us about your parents and what impact they had on your early life?

Schuller
Yes. My father and mother were, by all standards I guess, poor. They owned or were buying a farm and they were farming people. That meant they were always able to live with faith because the farmer always has something to look forward to. He plants his seeds and has a harvest.

Depression happens when we don't have anything to live for. That's why farmers are believers in God, because they watch their seed sprout and new plants grow.

Wright
In 1955, with $500 in your pocket, you and your wife started a church. I understand that it took tremendous faith for both of you. What really impressed me, however, was the fact that you knocked on 3,500 doors to learn what the residents wanted. That was an enormous task.

Do you believe that somewhere within the definition of faith lies a charge to do the work necessary for success?

Schuller
I had a whole year to do it. But, absolutely, that is the heart of what faith must be.

Wright
I've been a salesman most of my life. I've been selling for years and years and anyone who does that much research and door-knocking deserves to be successful.

You have referred to yourself as a "Christian Capitalist." Can you tell our readers what you mean?

Schuller

Well, I believe that people should try to achieve self-esteem and hopefully, independence—and freedom is the core of that. In the United States of America, we are free to achieve financial independence. It's not against the law as it would be in a pure socialist state or a pure communist state.

Christian Capitalism is a principle of acquiring your own wealth. Capitalism without the principles that I find in Christianity can be as bad as communism or anything else because it can generate greed, deception, theft, murder—you name it. Capitalism is very dangerous, just as freedom is very dangerous without a set of personal morals and ethics.

I say a Christian Capitalist lives on three principles: *One:* earn all you can. Don't make it by trying to win the lottery. You have no pride of achievement if you go about it that way. *Two:* invest all you can. *Finally:* give all you can.

Wright

As I prepared for this interview, I was struck by a prayer that you wrote titled *Success*. In it you wrote this: *Faith stimulates success. Hope sustains success. Love sanctifies success.*

Would you comment on Faith, Hope, and Love as it relates to your success?

Schuller

Well, nobody is going to be a true success, meaning satisfied with his or her accomplishments and living proud with the way that it, was done unless that person lives by this trinity of faith, hope, and love.

Wright

Dr. Schuller, as a pastor of the largest RCA church, you were a part of the United States delegation to the funeral of the universally loved Mother Teresa in Calcutta. You stated that she was the "first lady of the twenty-first century."

When did you first meet Mother Teresa and what impressed you the most about her faith in God?

Schuller

What I think impressed me most about her faith in God was that she was a happy person. She smiled. When I stepped off the President's plane in Calcutta for the funeral, the first huge billboard we saw was her picture with the line, "Smile. It's the beginning of peace." I think I first met her through the writings of a now-deceased friend in England, who became a Christian through her. Then, of course, I visited her home of the dying in Calcutta thirty years ago.

Wright

The Crystal Cathedral is known worldwide for its architectural excellence. Will you tell us about how it came to be and a little about its design?

Schuller

Yes. Well, I started this church, as you mentioned, with no money and couldn't find a hall to rent. I knew I had gifts because I was elected to Phi Beta Kappa in college, and national honor fraternities, so I knew I had talents and gifts, but I needed a place to speak. I couldn't find an empty hall anywhere.

Finally, I went to a drive-in theater and the guy there said that I could talk from the snack bar rooftop and that's how I started. That would be my church home for over five years. Every Sunday when I prayed or read the Bible or heard religious music, all I could see were clouds and the sky and trees bending in the wind and birds flying. So, twenty years later when I needed a big church, I was homesick for the sky and said to the architect, "Why not make it out of all glass?" So, the Crystal Cathedral was born. It reflects where I came from as a child when I lived on the farm in the country and the sky was the most dominant thing.

Wright

When I was out at your church a few years ago, I remember one of the guides there was telling us something about the bricks. Instead of putting them horizontally, you had put them vertically. Is that true?

Schuller

It's not *really* true. It's true that Richard Noints was my first architect. Richard was probably the greatest architect for part of his life and he did the Tower of Hope and the cross on top of it. He did the Gallery and the first church that I had here. He said that he had always wanted to set stone vertically, but nobody would go along with it—but I did. So, the stone is set vertically here. It is a historic piece of architecture; we never use random stone, just the vertical stone. So, it's not bricks, it's stone.

As of this interview, the last building that we've just built is a glorious structure. I think it's outstanding. It's done by Richard Meyer. The Getty Museum is doing the Pope's chapel in Rome. This is the only piece of real estate in the United States of America where the buildings are all done by gold medal, F.A.I.A., world-class architects: Richard Noints', Tower of Hope, Phillip Johnson's Crystal Cathedral, and now Richard Meyers' International Center for Possibility Thinking. We've received a lot of press on it and are going to get a lot more.

Wright

When I visited your church it was at Christmastime; I was fascinated by everything I saw. Some of my most cherished memories were of the sculptures on the grounds. The statues of Pharisees and the adulterous woman spoke volumes to me. I didn't have to read the Bible to figure out what was going on.

Will you tell our readers where all the beautiful art came from?

Schuller

It came from me. I've been in charge of this place for forty-eight years. Since I started with nothing, I have the principle that everything makes a statement. A weed says something. A flower says something. Everything makes a statement. Sidewalks make statements. I put Bible verses in granite in the sidewalks so that people would just be walking and accidentally read a word from scripture that might reach them. Then I chose to take what, in my life and heart, are the most important themes in the Bible and turn them into sculpture. *"Let Him who is without sin cast the first stone,"* that's the woman convicted of adultery. The prodigal son—you know the story?

Wright

Yes.

Schuller

Okay, so that's been done. The lost sheep—that's been done. "Peace be still" is the sculpture of Christ calming the water. I picked what I call the most fundamental, historic, classical, powerful, positive principles taught by Jesus and put them in sculpture. They're all done by different sculptors. I had, I think, seven different artists do the work.

Wright

When you were talking a few minutes ago about earning as much as you can and investing as much as you can—of course the *Hour of Power* and all that you're able to do out there in Garden Grove just boggles the mind. I've been on a church staff for forty years and I just can't imagine how much all of that would cost weekly for you to be able to reach the entire world like you do.

Schuller

Well, we're on a $65-million budget.

Wright

Wow.

Schuller

The income is always challenging. We've never had a surplus. If we had a surplus, we'd put it into expanding the business.

What staff are you on?

Wright

I've been directing church choral music and I write choral music. As of this interview, I'm music director at the Kodak United Methodist Church here in Tennessee.

Schuller

Well, we've got a good choral conductor here.

Wright

I know. I listen all the time.

Schuller

The director of the Mormon Tabernacle Choir came to church here last week and he went to our director and said, "Boy, we would like to sing in that cathedral."

Wright

Well, as a matter of fact, while I was waiting for you to come to the phone, your secretary put me on hold. I was able to hear your choir sing for a minute or two.

Dr. Schuller, your *Hour of Power* reaches more than twenty million viewers weekly all over the world. You have the opportunity to have some of the most famous people in the world as guests at your church. Do your permanent members feel that they are really a part of a church that fills the need of your community and do they feel a closeness to each other?

Schuller

Not the way they should and that's why we had to open a new facility. That's the building we just opened. It cost me $40 million, it took seventeen years, and you've never seen anything like it. Nobody in church work has ever built anything like it. The front of it opens wide so that when you are in the courtyard, instead of looking at a back wall with power poles and houses over the fence, you're looking at the front of a gorgeous building. The wall totally opens up and you see the huge living room. It's like the lobby of a five-star hotel. There's a beautiful food court, which is just shocking in its beauty. So, it's a gathering place for the people and it's doing wonders.

Our congregation's attitude toward the *Hour of Power* is that they're assistant ministers. They meet the tourists who come here (a million a year). They sing in the choir for the *Hour of Power*. So, they feel a part of the community when they become a part of the four hundred "hospitality people" group. They feel a part of the community when they join the music in the church. They're a part of the community when they man the twenty-four-hour New Hope Telephone Counseling—the first counseling prevention ministry in the United States of America for thirty-four years.

So, organizations that do the ministry form their own sense of community and that's the way it's got to be. We also have small groups that meet. I don't know how many small groups we have, but they all look upon the local television ministry as our primary world missionary work, which it is.

Wright

But there's still a feeling of community.

Schuller

Only if they get into a small group or become one of the 3,000 members that form these working ministry groups. If they just come, sit in the pew, and go home, no, they don't feel like part of a community.

Wright

When I phoned recently, you were out inspecting some of the new construction. Are you saying it's on the same location?

Schuller

Oh yes, it is on the same location.

Wright

So, it's adjacent to the Cathedral?

Schuller

Yes. The three buildings form a triangle. The new building is reflected in the mirrored Cathedral and it can be viewed from the Tower of Hope. If you go through the new building, it is a museum that motivates. The view in architecture is the most important thing. We don't have a mountain or a lake or a river view here, but what we do have is a view of two buildings that are world-famous for the art of their architecture. Those two buildings are the stunning view from the new building. Nobody has ever seen it until now because there were houses, power poles, and telephone poles. The west side of the buildings is the most beautiful and now they're seen for the first time.

Wright

I just can't wait to see it.

Schuller

You would never know the place. It is stunning. We won first prize in the State of California for our landscaped gardens.

Wright

I came to Anaheim one time to do a speech on presentation skills for professional speakers and I drove to the Cathedral. It was at Christmastime and angels were flying around in the air—I couldn't believe it—and the orchestra was excellent. You are just so fortunate to have so much to work with there.

Schuller

I tell you, I am. I've been so fortunate to get the best people in the world to become my friends and they made it great—like Mary Martin, did you ever hear of her?

Wright

Oh, yes.

Schuller

All right, Mary Martin was on the cover of *Life Magazine* seven times. She flew as Peter Pan. When I was putting together *The Glory of Christmas*, she said that I should have angels and they should fly. She said she knew how to do that and she took charge of it. She got the guy in here to make it happen and that's why we were the first church with flying angels.

Wright

I had no idea. Of course, Mary Martin and people like Ethel Merman are the grand ladies of Broadway.

Schuller

She's dead now, of course.

Wright

Yes, unfortunately.

Dr. Schuller, you have acknowledged that the Rev. Dr. Norman Vincent Peale was one of your mentors.

Schuller

Yes, he was a pastor of our first church in America. That church was founded by fifty-four Dutch colonists in 1628, who bought the land from the Indians. We are the oldest corporation with an unbroken ministry in the United States, secular or sacred.

Wright

What do you think makes a great mentor? In other words, are there characteristics that mentors seem to have in common?

Schuller

First of all, is excellence—they excel in their chosen career or field. That's the number one thing. They also have to respect and love the person they mentor as someone they think has talent and possibilities. When you've got those two going, then you're on your way.

Wright

If you could have a platform, Dr. Schuller, and give our readers advice on how to develop their faith in God in order to live a richer, fuller, more meaningful life, what would you say?

Schuller

I would tell them that the most important thing is to believe in the cosmic being that the Bible calls God. This God is personal, meaning He can think. He's not just a cosmic force or nothing to be admired at all. You can't admire electricity. You can be thankful for it, but you can't admire it. God is intelligent, He is affectionate, and He is eternal. He is part of eternity.

The question is then how to develop an awareness of who He is and what He is like. The answer I give is: Jesus Christ. That's why Jesus Christ is the heart of my faith. Whether you are Protestant, Catholic, Jewish, or Muslim, you know that He believes in God. That's why I believe in God. How do I know I'm right? I cannot believe that Jesus Christ was wrong. No way. If I think that I'm smarter than Jesus was when it comes to things like prayer and faith in God, then I'm the world's worst egotist and the person most lacking in humility.

I think I'm living by Jesus' teachings and His claim to be the Son of God—the Savior. I'm living by it. I tell you, at the time of this interview I'm close to seventy-seven, my faith in God has given me a fabulous life—God has given me a fabulous life. Just look around me. Look what we've done. I know that it has all come from God and from Jesus.

Wright

I certainly can see the fruits of His labor every time I look at the television station and see a beautiful edifice there that just really reaches people all over the world.

I really appreciate the time you have taken with us today. I wish you continued success, of course, in leading people to Christ. I think that you are one of the great men of God. Again, I appreciate the time that you have spent with me today.

In 1968, DR. SCHULLER founded New Hope, the world's first live, church-sponsored twenty-four-hour counseling and suicide prevention hotline. Since its inception, it is estimated that over a million people have dialed this hotline and received immediate counseling.

The Garden Grove congregation continued to grow and when a larger building was needed, Rev. Schuller commissioned the renowned architect Philip Johnson to build a new building, all of glass. It became known as the Crystal Cathedral. After almost insurmountable difficulties, this 2,736-seat architectural marvel was dedicated in 1980, "To the Glory of Man for the Greater Glory of God." Today, one million people visit the Cathedral annually, for regular Sunday worship, for conferences, seminars, workshops, and for two annual pageants, "The Glory of Christmas" and "The Glory of Easter."

Dr. Schuller is the author of more than thirty books, six of which have found a place on the New York Times and Publishers Weekly bestseller lists. Robert and Arvella Schuller have five children, all active in Christian ministry.

Dr. Robert Schuller
Crystal Cathedral Ministries
13280 Chapman Avenue
Garden Grove, California 92840
Phone: 714.971.4000

Francine Ivey

My story of *amazing faith*, although unlike many of the incredible stories in this book, is probably like most of yours. I do not have a devastating accident or tremendous loss to tell you about. My need for amazing faith is in the normal, daily things of life—paying bills, raising kids, and juggling an ever growing schedule and to do list—*a list that is longer than any person can get done in one lifetime!*

Sure, I have had many times when my faith was tested and I would have to stand in faith when I wanted to crumble. I remember the ride in an ambulance when my eldest daughter, Reagan, had a seizure in my arms. I cried out for God to heal her. I remember when it seemed the bills never met the budget and I prayed believing that God was my provider. I remember being in an accident when I was seven months pregnant with my son, Gracen, and I went into labor way too early. I remember the time we rushed our six-week-old baby, Peyton, to the hospital where she laid in an oxygen tent for five days because of a virus called RSV. I will never forget when I found out my mother and my husband's mother were both diagnosed with cancer—the same week my husband's father passed away.

Each time I prayed for God to intervene. What I describe is *life* and when life gets tough—and it always does—that is when we need *amazing faith!*

A Faith that goes beyond Your Circumstance!

For great is your love, reaching to the heavens;
Your faithfulness reaches to the skies.—Psalm 57:10

In order to have a true faith that will truly change your life, there are things you must know. First, faith does not mean believing in something long and hard enough that it finally just happens—faith must have an object it points to. When you say you have "faith in your son" as he backs out of the driveway with your car for the first time, you are saying that you know from your experience he is able to drive carefully. He has shown you that he is responsible enough to care for your car. Your faith is based on your son's character, not in *your ability* to believe in him.

The same is true with faith in God. Our faith must be based on knowing Him in a personal way. He is not obedient to our faith—our faith is a testimony to His character. You see, when I go through situations in my life that I do not understand, I draw on the fact that I know my God is able to do mighty and awesome things and that He loves and cares for me.

So I don't sit there trying to believe enough or will something into existence. I stand. I stand because I *know* my God and my Savior. I know that Jesus proved His love, His goodness, and His ability through the very act of the cross.

He proved His *love* by dying for me,
His *goodness* by forgiving me,
And His *ability* when he rose from the dead,
    conquering both death and the grave.

I would like to have the resolve to stand firm like the woman I call "the woman of great faith," in Matthew chapter 15 of the Bible. There are only two people in the Bible whose faith Jesus praised and she is one of them. Her story is an amazing story, though I didn't understand it at first. In the story Jesus was acting so out of character—not at all like the Savior I knew—but He knew this women's heart and He knew what amazing faith she had. I believe He desired to show that kind of faith to His disciples. So He put her to the test.

The woman came to Jesus because her daughter was demon possessed. The Bible says, "He answered her not a word." Then the disciples told Jesus to send her away because she was bothering them.

(Have you ever felt this way? It seems that your prayers are not heard and the church, your family, and your friends act like you're bothering them.)

She does not give up, she pleads with Jesus again. He then tells her He was not sent for her. (She is a Gentile—a Canaanite woman.) The Bible says she fell down and worshiped Him, asking again for Him to help her. (Have *you* ever felt the urge to worship when things are falling apart and it seems God is not listening to you? That is definitely not my natural reaction.)

Jesus then said, "It is not good that I give the children's bread to the little dogs." (I am afraid that at this point I would have failed the test.) She doesn't even seem to flinch. She knows that He is good even when it doesn't appear that way. She knows that He loves her, no matter what is going on and she knows He is able to heal her daughter. So she responds with *amazing faith.* "Yes, Lord, but even the little dogs eat the crumbs from the master's table." Wow! It is then that Jesus bursts with pride and exclaims, "Oh woman, great is your faith! Let it be to you as you desire!" Her daughter was healed that very hour!

How could she stand for so long? How could she take so much? Because she had a faith that was not based on circumstance, her feelings, or even what others might think. It was based on what she knew about Jesus! So no matter what happened or how she might feel at the time, she knew she could trust *Him,* and because she trusted Him it didn't matter what the moments held or how He appeared to be acting. She stood, unwavering, and the Son of God took notice and with pride He let everyone know what an amazing faith she had!

When Your Faith Wavers

Immediately the father of the child cried out and said with tears,
Lord, I believe; help my unbelief!—Mark 9:24

Sometimes it seems that even the most faith-filled children of God find themselves in situations that shake their faith. In some situations or at sometimes in my life I find my faith strong. I seem ready to take on the world! Then at other times I feel weak like a babe in my walk with Christ. There I am easily shaken. I believe we can find our answers to why this may happen to us in Mark, chapter 9.

Here we see a story about a father who brought his son to Jesus' disciples to heal him. They could not. When Jesus arrived and the father told Him what had happened, He responded, "O faithless generation, how long shall I be with you? How long shall I bear with you? Bring him to me." (verse 19). The father brought his son to Jesus. Jesus looked at the father and said, "If you can believe, all things are possible to him who believes." Here is where I love the father's candidness and honesty. The Bible says the father cried out, "Lord, I believe; help my unbelief!" Jesus then rebuked the spirit that had held this young man since childhood and immediately the boy was healed!

In this story the disciples are the same disciples who had earlier healed many. They had cast out demons and set people free. What had changed? Why were they struggling? The father must have had faith or he would not have brought his son in the first place. Now he is struggling.

I think this passage shows us why. First, failure breeds doubt. The disciples had failed. We find out later it is because they had not fasted and prayed (verse 29). You see, sometimes things don't happen quickly for us or it's the kind of situation God requires our obedience and faithfulness and we get discouraged and doubt will creep in.

I used to struggle with anxiety. I would wake up at night in a full panic. I believed I was dying. I could reason with myself about how ridiculous this was but it did not matter. Those of you who have experienced this condition understand what I am saying. There is no reasoning with it. Everything that you feel is as real to you as the sky above and ground beneath your feet. I prayed for healing. The next night there I was again fighting with my own thoughts and fears. I again prayed for healing and once again the following night, I was in a full panic attack. I remember talking with God. I searched for every scripture on healing and faith. Then God remind me of all the times before when He had immediately stepped into my life and answered my prayers. He then explained how at times He would require more from me. I would need to stand—and I did! Night after night I would pray and plead with Him. I would quote scripture that He had directed me to find and stand upon. Then one day . . . it was gone!

You see, when the disciples had failed it caused them to doubt in both themselves and God and it shouldn't have. Sometimes it takes more than one prayer, even one filled with faith! Sometimes it takes an all-out war to win, but I have found that in *Christ we always win.*

The second thing in this passage that will defeat our faith we find in verse 14. The disciples are arguing with the scribes.

If you choose to surround yourself with a crowd of people you continually have to defend your faith to, you will never have a strong faith. You must surround yourself with people who will strengthen your faith. Although there are times when someone who challenges your beliefs will strengthen your faith, a constant diet of that will surely diminish it.

> *Casting down arguments and every high thing*
> *that exalts itself against the knowledge of God,*
> *bringing every thought into captivity*
> *to the obedience of Christ.—2 Corinthians 10:5*

Make sure you have friends who will encourage you to believe—those who can share testimonies of how God moved in their own lives. The Bible says we will defeat the devil by the blood of the Lamb and the word of our testimony (Revelation 12:11). We can defeat fear, doubt, and unbelief with Jesus and by sharing our testimonies with one another. So choose your conversations wisely. Don't get into vain arguments and disagreements.

The Power of No Faith

> *Now He did not do many mighty works there*
> *because of their unbelief.—Matthew 13:58*

Satan knows the power of "no faith" and you should too. When Jesus was in Nazareth He performed very few miracles there—they had no faith.

It is amazing to me how an Almighty God, who created the universe, put the stars in place, tells the sun and moon when to rise and set, will allow us the freedom to choose our paths in life. Our faith in Jesus Christ activates the power of God in our life, as well as the lack of faith will prevent it.

I have three beautiful children and all of them are very different. My firstborn, Reagan, is my conservative child. She is cautious and sensible. My second child, Peyton, is energetic and adventurous. She had a dislocated elbow before she was four. She would take flight from one bunk bed to the other and one evening she didn't quite make it. She is the first to try things and the first to say, "I can do it!" My third child, Gracen, is only eighteen months old so I am not sure but I believe he also is quite adventurous. He might be a lot like his grandfather—my father—who decided to parachute off the roof of their home with an umbrella! It should be an interesting next eighteen years!

My husband, Wade, and I took Reagan to an amusement park where we ended up standing in front of go-carts. My husband was quite enthusiastic to share this experience with our daughter. She, on the other hand, was terrified. She latched on to his neck and would not let go. We talked, encouraged, fussed, and even bribed her to get her to try it. We knew if only she would try, she would enjoy it so much; but there was nothing we could do to convince her.

We left that day disappointed. We knew that she had missed out on something so wonderful—something she would have enjoyed immensely. She is now eleven and loves to drive go-carts, riding lawnmowers, and four-wheelers. She is constantly reminding me that she would like a mustang convertible the day she turns sixteen! That day in the amusement park is long forgotten but it does teach us a valuable lesson when we are discussing faith.

You see, fear is faith's greatest enemy and just like my daughter we can miss out on so much when we do not trust God and place our faith in Him. God is always at work in the world. Miracles are happening everywhere. His hand and Spirit move all over the earth. It is our faith that put us in the middle of all that. So many stories in the Bible show us this.

The woman with the issue of blood and the story Jairus, the synagogue leader, in Luke 8:40–56 are good examples of this. The woman reached out and touched the hem of Jesus' garment and she was healed instantly. Jesus stopped to see who had touched Him. We find out that a crowd of people were around Him that day. Many were touching Him but only one touch accessed the power of God.

In the story of Jairus' daughter we read that she dies while Jesus is on the way to the house and Jesus reminds Jairus to believe. When He arrives at the house the mourners are already gathering. He tells them not to cry because she is not dead. They laughed and ridiculed Him and *He puts them outside!* (Can you imagine that? God is about to raise this little girl from the dead and you are outside because you had no faith.)

That is exactly what happens to many of us. The power of God is around us every day. He is at work everywhere but our decisions affect where we are. Sometimes, like the Pharisees and Sadducees, we are there but we are spiritually blind. They had been looking for the Messiah, yet because of their own agenda and their fear of losing power and control they could not even see their promised salvation right in front of them. It was fishermen and tax collectors who recognized Jesus.

I desire to have the faith to be a part of all that God is doing around me, not to be a critic or walk in fear. I want to have the faith that accesses the power of God. I hope I never have to be put outside when God wants to do something miraculous!

If you never see the hand of God move, if you are one of those in church who look glazed over, who never receive anything from the sermons, and you are bored or agitated by the worship, and if you get more excitement from a business meeting than in Sunday morning worship, you may have no faith and you are missing so much. You need Amazing Faith!

Producing Amazing Faith in You

I have come that they may have life,
and that they may have it more abundantly.—John 10:10b

So how can you have amazing faith—the kind that activates the power of God in your life? I have found there are eight steps to amazing faith:

1. *You must have a personal relationship with Jesus Christ.* Your faith must have an object. Faith alone will change nothing. Faith in Christ changes everything. You must start by giving your life to Him and placing your faith in Him, then you can begin your journey to amazing faith!

2. *Ask.* (See Matthew 7:7; Luke 11:9.) The Bible tells us to ask. It says we have not because we ask not. So go to Him and ask Him to give you a faith that the Bible describes as a faith that will move mountains!

3. *Choose your friends wisely.* (See Numbers 13, the story of Joshua and Caleb.) Who are you listening to? The Israelites in the Old Testament chose to listen to the ungodly spies who told them they could not defeat the giants in the Promised Land. They chose to believe the spies' bad report instead of God's promise and they paid the price—they wandered in the desert for forty years. Although their children inherited the Promised Land, they never entered. Be careful who gives you advice and who you choose to influence your decisions. It may cost you more than you know.

4. *Know the Word of God.* (See Psalm 119:105.) You will find

the truth in every situation in the Bible. When you depend on how you feel or on the circumstances of life around you, you lose faith. Just like Peter when he was walking on the water with Jesus, as long as he kept his eyes on Jesus he was fine, but the moment he looked around at the waves of the storm he sank. Let God keep you focused on Him through the scriptures and you will find yourself walking on water in the middle of the storm!

5. *Worship.* Learn to worship Him. It is through our worship that we get a true sense of who God is and the magnitude of His power and majesty. Through our worship we focus on who He is and in doing so we find that our needs and problems are a lot smaller than He is.

6. *Choose faith, not feelings.* Sometimes it just boils down to our choosing to believe, no matter what our feelings are saying or the circumstances and situations around us. Most people are led by their feelings and find themselves tossed to and fro in the storms of life. I have found that when I focus on the truth, no matter what I feel, that my feelings will then follow. Choose to believe even when you don't *feel* it!

7. *Do not ask amiss.* James 4:3 says, "You ask and do not receive because you ask amiss, that you may spend it on your pleasures." Sometimes we do not see God at work because we want to dictate the way He works. We must remember: He is God—we can ask for what we desire but ultimately we must leave it with Him. God is not on trial in our lives. He is good, He does love us, and He is able to do exceeding and mighty things for and through us, but we must trust Him to do what is best, at the right time, and in the right way.

8. *Persistence.* Over and over the Bible talks about persistence and finishing. I believe many times we don't see God because we don't persevere—we give up too early. Sometimes, like the "woman of great faith," we have to stand. Don't give up. God is worthy of your persistence and I am sure your request is too important to give up on.

God intends and expects His children to live an abundant and extraordinary life full of favor and blessing. It is not always easy but as children of God we are never alone. In John 10:10, Jesus tells us why

He came—He came to give us an abundant life. The only one who can stop this in your life is you. No one else can.

Choose to have faith—*amazing faith*. Ask Him for it, be careful what or who may have your ear. Memorize and study the Bible because there you will find the truth in every situation. Take time to worship, magnify, and exalt Jesus. Don't be led by your feelings, and when you ask for something, don't have your own agenda.

Let God be God. Your faith is in Him, so trust Him and never, ever give up! Then you will have *amazing faith* and when you do, you will have an *amazing life!*

FRANCINE IVEY is the founder of King's Daughter Ministries and co-founder of WFI Empower Ministries. She is a wife, mother of three, worship leader, national women's speaker, and author. Her husband, Dr. Wade Ivey, is a gifted multi-denominational pastor, worship leader, and evangelist. For seventeen years, Francine has been a pastor's wife, women's minister, and worship leader. She now serves at Empower Ministries in Mobile, Alabama.

Francine was raised in the military and traveled worldwide. At age eight, she first heard God's call and at twenty-one, on her wedding day, she gave her whole heart and life to Jesus!

Francine Ivey
King's Daughter Ministries
P.O. Box 768
Theodore, AL 36590
Phone: 251.402.1571 Office: 251.602.8515
E-mail: francine@wfiministries.org
www.wfiministries.com

Harold Dennis

On May 14, 1988, in Carrolton, Kentucky, the worst drinking and driving crash in U.S. history occurred, killing twenty-seven of my closest friends. I was fourteen years old at the time, and most of the victims of the crash were around the same age.

I remember it as if it had happened yesterday. It was a beautiful, spring Saturday morning. My sister and my friends and I couldn't wait to enjoy a day of fun and fellowship with one another. That morning, we headed up to King's Island, an amusement park in Cincinnati, Ohio. Just as we had anticipated, the day was filled with smiles, laughs, roller coasters, and funnel cakes. Little did we realize, as this day would end, our lives would change forever.

On our way home, back to Radcliff, Kentucky, a drunk driver in a pick-up truck was traveling on the wrong side of Interstate 71. At approximately 10:55 PM the truck and the bus collided, puncturing the gas tank and engulfing the bus with flames.

I was sitting in the fifth seat from the front next to my best friend Andy, who was asleep against the window and a friend I had met that day, Aaron, who was next to the isle. Exhausted from the long day, I was asleep also at the time of the impact. I remember waking up to the sound of loud screams and tires screeching and squealing. Terrified and still not aware of what had occurred, I knew that I had to get out of that bus to stay alive. I tried to get out of the nearest window and was unsuccessful. At that point, not fully realizing what I was doing, I ran toward the front exit of the bus directly into the flames.

It was at this point when I knew that there was only one way out of the bus—the rear exit. I had a choice: I could give up or I could fight for my life and go toward the rear of the bus, and that's what I did. In the pitch black darkness of night and the unbearable heat and smoke, I began climbing over the seats and bodies in front of me, fighting my way to the back of the bus.

As I reached the rear exit of the bus, I was met by several other people fighting for their lives and bodies that were piled from the floor all the way to the ceiling. Sixty-seven people—one exit. It was by the grace of God that I was pulled from the bus by a rescuer. As I hit the ground outside the bus, I remember just running as fast as I could to safety, hearing explosions in the background, and thanking God that I was alive. As a result of this fatal crash, I suffered third degree burns to my face, shoulder, and back. I also suffered severe lung damage from the carbon monoxide and smoke inhalation.

People often ask me if my views on life are different because of what happened on May 14, 1988. My answer is a resounding *"abso-lutely*—I think!" Let me explain. When you really think about it, what views on "life" could I have possible had at age fourteen? I didn't have a lot of worldly views or views on life at that age. What fourteen-year-old does? So, in reality, I don't know if my views are any differ-ent than they would have been had this crash not occurred. But what I do know as a result of what happened that day is that tomorrow is never promised. Our lives can change in an instant and without no-tice. In some cases, there may not be a tomorrow. Although it is not very realistic for us to live every day as if it were our last, I cannot stress enough the importance of not taking life for granted.

I have had the distinct honor of sharing my story with thousands of people. The audience generally has varied from elementary school kids to church groups to college students to professionals. My mes-sage to these folks is simple: have a plan, put it into motion, and per-severe. Although this message relates to all facets of one's life, I use my experiences in the nation's worst drinking and driving accident and how those experiences changed my life forever to illustrate the power of perseverance.

I was on my death bed at age fourteen. I spent two months in the hospital and I have had numerous reconstructive surgeries, eyebrow implants, and a complete ear reconstruction because my left ear was completely burned off. I don't share these things with people for sym-pathy, but to illustrate the struggle—both physically and mentally—that other burn victims and I have gone through.

I firmly believe that struggle builds character. I believe that God put me in that seat that night and spared my life for a reason—He has a plan for me and *my* plan is to seek out *His* plan and execute it.

Let me talk about one of those plans that I think God had, and still has for me. Before this accident occurred, I was a pretty good athlete. I started playing soccer at age six and played a little baseball as well, but soccer was my main sport. I was always blessed with great hand-eye-foot coordination and with raw foot speed. These attributes naturally helped me become successful as a young soccer player.

Well, as you can understand, after being nearly dead and in critical condition for several days and spending two months in the hospital suffering from life-threatening burns and lung damage, my future in athletics no longer looked very bright. The probability of my participation in organized sports was very low. Despite that low probability, I had a different plan. I had a "voice"—my voice—telling me that the only thing stopping me from returning to sports was me. Have a plan, put it into motion, and persevere. That's what I did.

I worked hard every day doing physical therapy and training (on my own) to get my mind and body back in the shape it was in before the accident. As a result, I was able to not only make my high school soccer team, but to become the second leading scorer on the varsity team during my junior season, and the leading scorer on the team during my senior season. That same year I made the All-State Team as one of the best players in the state of Kentucky.

I didn't stop there. I decided to try out for the track team for the first time, made it, and competed in the 100 meter, 200 meter, 400 meter, 400mx1 relay, 400mx4 relay, and high jump. We became State Champions that year. I didn't stop there. I decided to try out as a place kicker for the football team. I made it, and became an All-District kicker. My point is this: despite the tragedy and the physical setbacks, my faith in God and His plans for me allowed me to accomplish these goals.

God has certainly blessed my life. Despite all of the daily struggles of facing society with the burns on my face, and still trying to adapt to life after the crash, I was able to complete a very successful high school athletic career and even carry it over into college. I received numerous offers from across the state to play collegiate soccer and finally accepted an offer from the University of Louisville in 1992 where I played for one year. After leaving the university in 1992, God led me to the University of Kentucky where He apparently had another plan for me.

Although getting my education from the University of Kentucky was extremely important to me, so was challenging myself physically and getting back to what God has always meant for me to do—to compete. I walked on to the University of Kentucky football team, having never played the sport before (other than one year of kicking in high school), and became a two-year varsity letter-winner at wide receiver/kick returner, and the recipient of several national awards for courage in sports: the Arete Award for Courage in Sports, Gene Autry Award for Courage in Sports, Johnny Unitas Courage Award, and others. I was also featured in *Sports Illustrated* and *People* magazines for my accomplishments and overcoming tragedy.

I cannot emphasize enough the value of sports and competition and how the "team" concept translates over into real life. In sports, people with vastly different roles and positions are all persevering toward the same common goal. In other words, sports helped me understand the importance of finding a network of people with the same goals and aspirations as I had. In the various sports activities I participated in my teams worked together to achieve greatness. I went on to receive my BA in Education (Kinesiology) in 1997 from the University of Kentucky.

God is good.

I have been asked if being involved in the tragedy (specifically the resulting physical and mental scars) has helped or hurt my personal life and my business life. During the early stages of my recovery, I felt that it really hurt my personal life because I was still dealing with the scars and accepting the "cards" that God had dealt me. Several people shied away from me, and several others welcomed me with open arms. The common denominator, and the most important factor, was that I had accepted it. There is no doubt in my mind that I am a stronger person because of it.

With that being said, I feel as though being involved in the tragedy has helped make me a more aware and understanding individual, which in my opinion are very good traits to have both personally and in business. It is unfortunate but true that experiencing a tragedy builds inner strength and prepares one for future challenges that life may have in store. Today I am a successful real estate developer, investor, and general contractor. I feel equipped to face any challenge that being a business owner can provide.

One example of how God is working in my life is the opportunity I have to share my life story with millions of people on screen. I am currently in pre-production of a major motion picture about my life story titled *The Phoenix*. I was presented with this same opportunity in 1995 while I was a junior playing football at the University of Kentucky. I signed a contract with a production company from Los Angeles giving them the rights to my life story to pursue making the movie. Consequently, the NCAA suspended me from football and explained that as an amateur athlete, I could not make money based on my amateur status. They told me that in order to make the movie I would have to give up my senior year of football, which that was not an option I wanted to choose, so I ripped up the contract and prayed to God that the opportunity would present itself again. Here we are today, full circle, with that very opportunity available again to portray my life on screen.

God is good.

It is my faith in God and His love for me that has gotten me where I am today.

I have always grown up in the church but had never accepted Jesus Christ as my Lord and Savior and professed my faith—until February of 1988, approximately ninety days *before* the crash. In fact, I still have the paper certifying my baptism at Stithon Baptist Church in Radcliff, Kentucky, on February 13, 1988. I have asked myself these questions over and over throughout the past nineteen years: What if I had not stepped forward that day and accepted the Lord into my life? Would my fate be any different? Would I still be here today to implement God's plans for me? I'll never know the answer to those questions, but what I do know, is that I'm glad that I can even ask them.

Have a plan, put it into motion, persevere. God bless.

HAROLD DENNIS, JR., is from Radcliff, Kentucky, where he was a three-sport athlete at North Hardin High School (football, track, and soccer). Harold was recruited to play soccer at the University of Louisville (1992) where he stayed for one year before transferring to the University of Kentucky. It was there that Harold earned his BA in Kinesiology (1997) and became a two-year letter winner on the UK football team (1994–1996). Currently, Harold is Founder and active CEO of Arete Ventures Inc., a commercial construction and Real Estate development company in Lexington, Kentucky. Harold's story is the subject of a feature film in preproduction titled *The Phoenix.* Harold performs public speaking engagements focusing on Motivation, Goal-Setting, and Perseverance. Harold is married with three children: Jasmine, Trey, and Kylee.

Harold Dennis, Jr.
President/CEO
Arete Ventures Inc.
121 Prosperous Place #11B
Lexington, KY 40509
Office: 859.264.0264
Fax: 859.264.0251
www.areteventuresinc.com

Patti Foster

L ife can change in the blink of an eye.
On the evening of June 18, 2002, my life changed suddenly
with no warning. Trauma entered my life in a most unexpected way, and faith took on a leading role!

Naturally, when I was told the title of this book—*Amazing Faith*—
and then I was invited to write a chapter in it, I immediately had a
keen desire to pass along what I've learned and encourage others
along this journey we call "life." Might I say, faith is truly *amazing*
when it's put into "living color!" I look forward to our time together
during this chapter. ☺

For years, I've been a strong advocate of faith in God Almighty,
but since the summer of 2002, my faith has grown much deeper. It
has saturated my life beyond what I could have imagined. Do you remember that hymn, "The Solid Rock"? (The words were written by
Edward Mote and the music was composed by William B. Bradbury.)
The first verse and refrain goes like this:

"My hope is built on nothing less
Than Jesus' blood and righteousness.
I dare not trust the sweetest frame,
But wholly lean on Jesus' name.
Refrain:
On Christ the solid Rock I stand,
All other ground is sinking sand;
All other ground is sinking sand."

And, yet, another hymn comes to mind (hmm, my brain must be in "music-mode" today): "My Faith Has Found a Resting Place" (lyrics by Eliza E. Hewitt and music by André E. M. Gétry). Does this speak about "amazing faith" or what!

"My faith has found a resting place,
Not in device or creed;
I trust the ever living One,
His wounds for me shall plead.
Refrain:
I need no other argument,
I need no other plea,
It is enough that Jesus died,
And that he died for me."

I could go on and on about music and amazing faith. They have such an enormously deep bond! Music has a way of expressing our faith when words can go no deeper. It's a language in and of itself that God has given to us. And for this I am deeply grateful!

My walk with God began when I was a child, and through the years my faith has grown. It has grown and flourished over time. The greatest points of my spiritual growth have happened during the toughest times of my life. Trials and suffering have been the main classes in my "school of faith" that have matured me along the way.

The events of my life match God's Word, where Paul wrote to the believers in Rome: "And we rejoice in the hope of the glory of God. Not only so, but we also rejoice in our sufferings, because we know that suffering produces perseverance; perseverance, character; and character, hope. And hope does not disappoint us, because God has poured out His love into our hearts by the Holy Spirit, whom He has given us" (Romans 5:2b–5, NIV). My faith in God and my relationship with Him cause me to want to "give away what I've been given!"

These two words—"amazing faith"—fit together much like a hand in a glove. God's amazing grace covers us as we press on, day by day in our faith that is built on our amazing Father. (God is a God who *never* ceases to amaze us!) Webster defines *"amaze"* as a verb that means "to fill with great surprise or sudden wonder; astonish."

Again, I'm reminded of a hymn. George Beverly Shea wrote a hymn titled, "The Wonder of It All." The refrain is: *"O, the wonder of it all! The wonder of it all! Just to think that God loves me."* Then, it repeats these words. That's the gist of it! It's a wonder—an amazing wonder! Faith goes beyond the realm of making sense. It's very much like an IV tube that extends from God down to us, and that's simply amazing!

Faith and prayer walk hand-in-hand in the life a Christian. To me, personally, they have been two of my closest companions. They've walked alongside me during some crucial times of my life. James said to "consider it pure joy, my brothers, whenever you face trials of many kinds, because you know that testing of your faith develops perseverance. Perseverance must finish its work so that you may be mature and complete, not lacking anything" (James 1:2–4 NIV).

These are easy words to say, but hard words to live. In order to live out the truth of these verses, a believer has to have a commitment to God and a relationship with God. It won't always feel good or be easy. It's during times like these that prayer and faith take on a leading role and carry us through some dark days. Think of the old hymn, "What a Friend We Have in Jesus." (The lyrics were written by Joseph M. Scriven and the music was composed by Charles C. Converse.) The words of each verse are directly related to prayer:

"What a Friend we have in Jesus, all our sins and griefs to bear!
What a privilege to carry everything to God in Prayer!
O what peace we often forfeit, O what needless pain we bear,
All because we do not carry everything to God in prayer."

How amazingly true! God wants us to talk with Him about everything, because He is our refuge. Nothing we say "falls on deaf ears." God listens.

Helen Keller said, *"Character is not developed in quiet and ease. Only through experience of trial and suffering can the soul be strengthened, vision cleared, ambition inspired, and success revealed."* How true this is! It is during our most rigorous times that we grow the most. These seasons of our lives mature us and teach us wisdom.

On June 18th of 2002, when I was in a horrible traffic accident and suffered Traumatic Brain Injury (TBI), I wasn't able to pray for myself or anyone else. I had faith in God and a strong relationship with Him, but I could do nothing about it. I was helpless. I needed the faith of others and the power of their prayers to carry me through this most devastating time of my life.

As my story has clearly pointed out so far, faith is truly *amazing* to me. I fervently believe there is power in prayer! About a year after this tragic day—when I was once again able to live and breathe on my own again without the aid of machines or medicines—I remember saying to a television broadcaster friend who was interviewing me, "There is true power in true prayer that goes to God Almighty. He doesn't forget those prayers. Not only does He hear them, He never forgets them." (This interview can be seen and heard on my Web site: www.pattifoster.com)

While I was in the hospital and in a coma, my name was lifted to God in prayer by friends and family members throughout each day. People all over the world were praying for me. God heard those prayers! Countless numbers of people were living out the truth of Colossians 4:2, "Devote yourselves to prayer, being watchful and thankful" (NIV).

On that hot summer night in June, three other ladies and I were in a red Tahoe on our way to our last Bible study meeting in Tyler, Texas, before taking a summer break. We had stopped at a red light at the intersection of Highway 69 and FM344 in Smith County/Bullard, Texas, when a semi, pulling a trailer full of cars, rear-ended us. Here's how it happened:

That night, at six forty-five, as we reached this intersection, we were all talking and laughing. Heather, the youngest lady in the Bible study, was telling us about her high school senior trip to New York City. While we were stopped, I took off my seatbelt so I could check on some flowers that I had bought for all the ladies in the Bible study. Apparently, it was at this point that impact happened.

Our Tahoe had already come to a complete stop as the truck was approaching the intersection. None of us was aware of the impending danger. In fact, we later found out that his truck and trailer rig was clocked as going sixty-seven miles per hour! Naturally, we had no idea of what was about to happen to us. Suddenly, with no warning, the tractor-trailer rig plowed into the back of the Tahoe. Window glass and pieces of vehicles began to fly into the air, as tires shrieked and skidded across the highway and onto the grass.

The driver of the semi made a bad mistake. Frankly, he had no business getting behind the wheel that night! He was intoxicated with five different drugs, talking on his cell phone, and going well over the speed limit. He wasn't paying attention to anyone or anything. The road signs along the highway made no difference to him.

All four of us ladies in the Tahoe were greatly injured. The driver, who was pregnant with her first child, suffered a miscarriage. One of the other ladies was thrown to the back of the Tahoe. She continues to suffer much pain due to nerve damage.

The young lady (Heather) who was sitting in the front passenger's seat was forcibly jerked around in her seat, thrown back and forth against the dashboard and her chair. Because of this, her spinal chord was severely damaged and her liver was ruptured.

I, on the other hand, was ejected from the Tahoe. I had been sitting in the seat behind the driver. When the man rear-ended us, my body shot out like a missile through the back and the opposite side of the Tahoe. My head and body hit this area so hard and abruptly that the Plexiglas burst open! (By the way, might I add, this panel was *not* designed to be opened.)

People who were at the scene of the accident have told me what they experienced. One eyewitness told me that when my body flew out of the Tahoe, she was completely caught off guard. Why? Because, she said, my body didn't immediately fall down to the ground, nor did it go across and hit a tree or pole. Instead, it went *up* into the air. She went on to say that it was as though the hands of God had come down and suspended me in the air above the very Tahoe that I had been in. When it had stopped spinning, that's when my body suddenly plummeted to the ground. I landed on the highway in a lane of traffic. But thankfully, the traffic had stopped when the collision occurred.

Another eyewitness, who was a registered nurse, saw my body thrown out of the Tahoe and into the air. She said that she thought I was a piece of laundry. Naturally, she was astounded when she realized it was not merely a piece of laundry, but my body!

Within seconds, state authorities and medical personnel appeared on the scene. They began responding to the traffic catastrophe that had just happened. A large crowd of people surrounded the area and began helping as much as possible. This was a very busy intersection!

Air 1, the emergency helicopter rescue program of East Texas Medical Center (ETMC) in Tyler, Texas, landed at the accident site within minutes. The crew quickly jumped out and loaded both Heather and me onto the same helicopter. We were taken directly to the Emergency Room of ETMC.

The medical team worked on Heather with incredible diligence. Her spinal chord had been severed and her liver had burst on impact. They did all that they could do, but to no avail. Unfortunately, late that night, the doctor met with her family and informed them that she didn't make it.

In that dismal hour of that hot summer night, the decision was made to disconnect Heather from all the machines and tubes. The staff moved her to a private room and allowed her family and friends to have some privacy with her, as they said their final farewell.

The trauma unit continued their struggle to keep me alive. Surgical procedures were performed. Different kinds of machines were hooked up to me. Tubes were everywhere. Because of all the deep lacerations and wide, open wounds, my body was covered with stitches, bandages, and everything else it required to keep my body together and in one piece.

They worked on me throughout the night and into the wee hours of the morning. The first seventy-two hours were the most critical—they weren't sure if I'd be able to make it. It was a dreadfully dire time. With all of their medical expertise and experience, the staff very well knew that a body could withstand only so much trauma. And this degree of traumatic injury was definitely beyond "so much." However, they were committed to doing their best!

I was given constant medical attention. In addition to multiple fractures and abstruse cuts and abrasions, I also suffered severe head trauma. My brain had been traumatically injured during the accident. Due to such severe trauma, I went into a coma, which lasted for about six weeks.

I have no recollection of this stage of my life. What I know is what I've learned from doctors, nurses, family, and friends. I don't remember any of my life from the moment I turned to check on the flowers that were behind my seat in the SUV until more than six weeks after the accident had happened. I have no memory of the crash, the scene, my being ejected from the Tahoe, etc. And, I must say, I consider this a merciful blessing of protection from the Lord. His promise was being lived out: "Even though I walk through the valley of the shadow of death, I will fear no evil, for You are with me; Your rod and Your staff, they comfort me" (Psalm 23:4 NIV).

I was in a coma the entire time that I was at ETMC in Tyler. After having been there for five and a half weeks, they released me and transported me, via ambulance, to Baylor Rehab in Dallas. Granted, those five and a half weeks of my recovery don't exist in my memory.

After having been at Baylor Institute for Rehabilitation (BIR) for about seven to ten days, I began to "wake up" and come out of the coma. I wondered where I was. I didn't know anything tragic had happened. I had no idea that we had had a wreck and such bad things had happened. I couldn't believe it—*we had been run over by a semi, pulling a trailer of cars? Really? Hmm . . .*

BIR was the main ingredient that God used to teach me how to live again. It wasn't an easy task. Every minute of every day took everything I had! I lived with constant pain, and it was excruciating to me, especially my neck and head. It was more than I could bear, but thankfully, nurses brought me medicine on a regular basis. Throughout my stay at BIR, they took incredibly good care of me!

Because of my severe head trauma, I had lost virtually all of my normal bodily functions. I couldn't swallow, chew, eat, see out of my right eye, walk, or talk. Living was extremely hard for me!

In time, as I underwent daily therapy sessions, I began to re-learn how to live again. The therapy sessions involved targeted and focused rehabilitation segments. At BIR, I was assigned a Social Worker (SW), Physical Therapist (PT), Occupational Therapist (OT), and a Speech Therapist (ST). Plus, a Neuropsychologist overlooked my case and stayed in touch with my parents. A Respiratory Therapist worked with me each weekday, and nurses took care of me every night and day.

Each weekday, my Occupational Therapist would come to my room and help me groom and get ready for the day. She would help me into the wheelchair and then push me down to the second floor of BIR where I would undergo my morning therapy session. At noon, I was pushed back to an elevator and returned to my room for lunch. After an hour or so, one of the Transporters would come by and take me back to the second floor for my afternoon therapy session.

My days were long and full. It was a rigorous schedule for me, but well worth every effort! Dr. Mary Carlile and Dr. Frank Smith were my doctors at BIR. They were wonderful and attentive! They and my therapists did their best to make my recovery as successful as it could be. They were positive and supportive, yet challenging and demanding. In other words, they were both tough and tender. They encouraged me and the other patients to keep trying and *not* give up! Well, they convinced me, and I tried as hard as I could to do everything they told me!

For about a month, God used Baylor Institute for Rehabilitation in a leading way to bring forth a "walking miracle" in me. BIR helped me to relearn how to do what other doctors said I would never again do!

God, most definitely, wasn't finished with me, yet! In fact, as I'm saying these words, I'm reminded of Jeremiah 33:3: "Call to me and I will answer you and tell you great and unsearchable things you do not know" (NIV). As prayer after prayer was being raised up to God for me, He was answering. His children were calling to Him, and He was listening to them.

After I had spent a month at BIR, I wasn't homeward bound yet. I was released and transported to a transitional rehabilitation center, which was located a couple of hours north of the DFW Metroplex. My parents, with the help and assistance of dear, sweet Ms. Ruthie of BIR, helped me get situated in their Toyota Avalon, and off we went! Safely and cautiously my dad drove us through the Dallas traffic and delivered me to Pate Rehab/Brinlee Creek Ranch in Anna, Texas. I remained there for over a month as an inpatient. After that time, I progressed into their outpatient program, where I remained for another month, until the end of October 2002.

While I was at Pate Rehab, I learned how to transition back into everyday living. It was hard work, but I was determined. Dr. Dickson, one of the directors of Pate Rehabilitation's Ranch location, reintroduced me to the genre of work that I had been doing before the wreck—speaking. Each week, he asked me to spend time in front of the patients in the conference room and speak to them. This was good practice for me! It gave me the opportunity to test my ability to remember things under pressure. Plus, it helped me to connect with people and try to get my point across to them in a personal and positive way. Each week, this practice enabled me to better relate to people and interact with them.

As I mentioned earlier, I was released from Pate Rehab at the end of October 2002. This was a significant step for me as a recovering head trauma survivor! I had begun to learn how to cope with life and deal with society. Leaving Pate was my first venture into the "land of the living."

As I continued to learn to live again, nonverbal communication began to play a major role in my life. The art of communicating, for me, was very difficult. There were many things that I didn't understand as I began to come out of the coma. For example, I was very confused by words. I didn't understand what many of them meant. It was impossible for me to stay focused and concentrate on anything for more than a couple of minutes, if that long. Life didn't make sense to me. Nothing really "connected" with me. In fact, the only thing that I was aware of was whatever my eyes could see at that very moment. In other words, if it wasn't in my view and I couldn't see it, I had no concept of it.

Kara Swanson, another recovering head trauma survivor, has written about what a tough time she had in her book, *I'll Carry the*

Fork. She said, "It was like being thrust into a foreign country with no road map, no way to speak the language, no directions home." As a head injury survivor, there was much of life that did not "compute" with me.

My brain had been so bruised and damaged in the accident. Every lobe had been hurt, some more than others. For example, my Temporal Lobes, which deal with understanding spoken words, were significantly damaged. Because of this, words really made very little sense to me. However, nonverbal communication did; I understood it well. As people came into my room, I immediately interpreted what they were saying nonverbally; otherwise, it seemed like a foreign language that I couldn't understand. For example, I paid attention to their:
eye contact
tone of voice
facial expressions
touch
body gestures, etc.

I better comprehended what was *not* being said, rather than what *was* being said. In essence, nonverbal communication was the most understood language to me and my traumatized brain.

At times, overwhelming obstacles have stared me in the face and tempted me to give up. Like most people, I've had those times when it's been really hard to "keep on keepin' on!" But in the midst of it all, I must say, encouragement has been one of the leading cheerleaders that God has used to help me continue along my journey! At various times, when I needed it most, God would cause someone to send me a wonderful dose of encouragement. It was, to me, much like vitamin B$_{12}$—it gave strength to my heart! For all of these times, I am truly grateful!

I'm reminded of Paul's words to the Hebrews, calling them to persevere: "And let us consider how we may spur one another on toward love and good deeds . . . let us encourage one another, and all the more as you see the Day approaching" (Hebrews 10:24–25b NIV). Cards, letters, surprise visits, and phone calls from dear friends and acquaintances made an indelible impression on my heart. Their thoughtfulness communicated love and support to me. My faith was bolstered and strengthened by them. At all of these different times, they, in fact, were really passing along encouragement to me through their faith in God.

This goes hand-in-hand with the theme of a classic Christian song that was recorded by Steve and Annie Chapman, "Faith of a Few Close Friends." When I was tired and down, people from all over the world took me to the Father in prayer. They shared their faith with me. Now, that's encouragement that nothing else can equal!

Plus, not only was I encouraged by the faith of so many different people, but my own personal relationship with Christ gave me hope.

One night, while I was at Pate Rehab, I sat down on my bed to read a bit before I turned off my light. As I picked up my Bible, it automatically fell open to Psalm 40. I began reading. The first verse spoke deeply to me—it "met me where I was." Here's what I read: "I waited patiently for the Lord, and He inclined to me and heard my cry" (Psalm 40:1 NKJV). I was reassured that God was listening to me, that He was keenly aware of all that I was going through.

Traumatic Brain Injury (TBI) didn't only affect me; it also took its toll on my family. I've talked with my mother about this and asked her how she made it through such a tough time. Here's what she said:

"The first thing that comes to mind is God. When you have a direct line, you don't have to wait for an operator. You get straight to the point with the Most Omnipotent God.

After God, friends come to mind. That night, I called a friend. She came and picked me up, and we headed for Tyler, Texas. (That's about twenty-eight miles north of us.)

When we arrived at ETMC (East Texas Medical Center), people were everywhere! Most of our friends had cell phones, and they began calling whomever I needed them to. (They were wonderful!) Patti's pastor was already there. (Amen!) Friends were there, day and night for the first seventy-two hours. That was the critical point. After we made it through this time, the people who came to support us remained there to comfort us.

We remained in the ICU at ETMC in Tyler for five weeks. We got to know the visiting hours and what nurses worked when. (Some of them remain friends still.) The doctors and nurses in the ICU were fantastic! They knew we were scared and nervous, so they would take time to explain things to us. It was quite an ordeal, but, praise God, He allowed Patti to stay with us!

Each visit in that room was heart-wrenching. The nurses had told us to say only positive things to her and not let her see or hear us cry. We kept music playing all the time. The nurses said they could tell it soothed Patti. (Patti graduated as a music major from Sam Houston State University in December of 1989.)

Patti remained on a ventilator until a few days before we were moved to Baylor Institute for Rehabilitation in Dallas. The doctors put a tracheostomy (trach) tube in her throat and a feeding tube into her stomach. As they rolled her out of her room in the ICU, she was conscious enough to wave "Good-bye" to the staff with her left hand. (Very moving!)

When we arrived at BIR, at the beginning of the week, Patti was placed in a ward that had five beds in it. Nurses monitored her constantly. They capped Patti's trach tube that Friday. On the following Saturday, Scott (her brother) and his wife, Rhonda, went to Dallas to be with Patti while my husband and I came home to take care of business. They heard her first words since the accident. (Another moving moment!) They called us on the phone and told us. (Amen and Amen!) To this day, her voice is still healing. Her left vocal cord lacks about 5 percent from being back to normal.

She still cannot sleep on her right side. Her head is very sensitive still. I said, "A thirty-four-year-old woman left my home on the evening of June 18, 2002. When she came out of the coma, I had a thirty-four-year-old baby." (A tough one to swallow!)

She had to learn how to talk, swallow, walk, write, think, and balance. When Patti was able to move out of the ward at BIR—one and a half weeks after she had been moved there—we got a private room with bath and fold-out chair/bed. I remained there with her for the rest of her time at BIR (four weeks). I got to know everyone very well. They were wonderful to us both. Patti progressed there very well.

Even though we were in Dallas, we still had faithful friends who came, called, sent cards, e-mails, etc. The nurses at both hospitals said they had never seen so much mail for one person. (Very uplifting!) I enjoyed it almost as much as Patti. (How do people get through life without God and friends? I never want to know!)"

God and the love and support of friends carried my family through this strenuous time, full of unknowns.

If you are a survivor of TBI, let me pass along some encouragement from my heart to yours! Immediately, three words come to my mind: *Don't give up!* When you think you're at the end of your rope, hang on! Keep trying! Don't be afraid to ask for help.

Above all, ask *God* for help—*pray!* He knows exactly what you're going through, what you're dealing with, how you're feeling, etc.—talk to Him. The Apostle Peter said, "Cast all your anxiety on Him because He cares for you" (I Peter 5:7 NIV). Don't hold back anything from God. He can withstand whatever you say to Him! And don't forget—listen to Him. He wants to talk with you, too! You matter to

Him.

To a family member of a TBI survivor, I encourage you strongly to "pray without ceasing," as the Apostle Paul urged the church of the Thessalonians. As I said to the TBI survivor, I also say to you: *Don't give up!* There is so much power in prayer, whether you're praying for yourself or someone else is praying for you. (This reminds me of a Christian song that has been recorded by a number of different artists, "Somebody's Prayin'.")

Seek out other parents and family members of TBI survivors and confide in them. Share ideas and experiences with them and ask them questions about what you're dealing with. In other words, talk to them and "get it off your chest."

Look for resources that can be of help to you. For instance, call your nearest Brain Injury Association (BIA) support group. Also, contact a rehabilitation institute and ask about its resource center. Look for books and information about traumatic brain injury (TBI).

In this stage of my recovery, helping other head injury survivors puts a smile on my face. Living out my motto, *M.A.D. Now! (Make A Difference Now!),* brings a gigantic smile to my heart! Letting God inspire others through me makes my heart go pitter-patter! There's a passage of scripture that has become very dear to me since all of this happened: "Let us not grow weary in doing good, for at the proper time we will reap a harvest if we don't give up. Therefore, as we have opportunity, let us do good to all people, especially to those who belong to the family of believers" (Galatians 6:9,10 NIV). So, lay hold of every opportunity God brings you. Let Him bless others through you. Serving others brings true success—success that makes a difference for God's sake and His Kingdom.

God's blessings to each of you as we travel along this journey we call "life." ☺

PATTI FOSTER'S experience in "connecting with people" started years ago (I won't tell you how many) when she was but a wee, little lassie. She's been a true "people-person" all of her life!

As a former radio personality, Patti is a dynamic advocate for TBI survivors. In 2002, she herself became a survivor of severe head trauma. With such purpose and ease, she spreads encouragement and inspiration to everyone she meets.

Patti, who is a member of International Speakers Network, travels full-time, touching lives through her speaking and writing ministries.

Patti Foster
Mobile: 903.445.6284
E-mail: patti@pattifoster.com
www.PattiFoster.com

Jennifer O'Neill

A Special Interview

David E. Wright (Wright)

Today we're talking with Jennifer O'Neill. She is an internationally acclaimed actress, film and television star, successful spokeswoman, composer, author, artist, proud mother of three, and (at the time of this interview) grandmother of four. Jennifer O'Neill has already accomplished enough for a lifetime. She began her international modeling career at the age of fifteen, after her family moved to New York from her native home of Rio de Janeiro, Brazil. Her career in the entertainment industry boasts many feature films including the classic *Summer of '42*, numerous television movies, and three television series. In addition, Jennifer held a thirty-year position as spokeswomen for Cover Girl Cosmetics. Following the success of her biography, *Surviving Myself*, Jennifer has written other books including, *From Fallen to Forgiven, You're Not Alone, A Fall Together, A Winter of Wonders,* and *A Late Spring Frost.* She also wrote a novel that was published by *Campus Crusade* titled, *Lifesavers.* She has served on the Board of Media Fellowship International.

Jennifer, welcome to *Amazing Faith.*

Jennifer O'Neill (O'Neill)

Thank you so much, David, it's my pleasure to be here.

Wright

All of us at Insight Publishing are excited about this project, Jennifer. To a person, all of us have been shaped by one or more remarkable woman—women such as our mother, a certain teacher, or a mentor. Although our authors won't admit it, we believe that they are remarkable women in their own right. I'm eager to explore this subject with you, but before we get down to the nitty-gritty, would you tell our readers what you've been up to lately?

O'Neill

David, sometimes when you ask for God's will in your life, you'd better put your seatbelt on. Often you find yourself doing things you never would have imagined. I have been so blessed since I wrote my first book, to have traveled on the speaking circuit. I have spoken to large groups with other women of faith—sometimes thirty thousand at a clip.

In 2002 I was the National Spokesperson for *Silent No More*, an awareness campaign, which deals with the issue of abortion and healing of abortion through God's grace. The campaign is fantastic and has made such a difference in the lives of women and families, healing through the grace of God.

I have also been blessed to have a platform to discuss various negative issues in my life that God has turned into positives. As it says in His Word, *"He will turn all things for good to those who love Him."* There are certain things and events that I have experienced in my life that have afforded me a platform to share some really wonderful news about God's grace and restoration. My speaking engagements take me to schools, colleges, the Senate and Congress, as well as to churches everywhere. I'm able to address the tough issues of teen suicide, abortion, and sexual abuse. (My daughter was sexually abused and she asked me to address that issue.) I also address domestic violence, depression, and other tough issues that many people experience. Very few of us side-step hard issues in life.

The good news is that God wants us healed, whole, existing in an enlightened state, and released though forgiveness and grace. It's there for all of us to have if we ask for it. It's all in Gods Word.

Traveling around the country speaking to women about women's issues, I see so many women who come up after I speak, usually in a flood of tears confessing an abortion they had or that they've been sexually abused or they're having difficulties with depression. I peel like an onion and let them know that they're not alone about certain issues. I love women. These are bright, vibrant, amazing women who in some areas of their lives are stuck in a shameful, guilty, fearful part of their past. None of those things are of the Lord and He is well capable and willing to heal us, if we bring those issues to Him.

Some time ago I decided to do a syndicated television series for women so that we can reach more women with this good news of what God offers us. It is titled, *Living Forever...More. Living Forever...More* is a half-hour, syndicated series in a one-hour Network special. At this time it appears as though it will not only be on syndicated television channels, but also on a new advanced channel on the Web. We hope to be reaching millions of women through this project.

We plan to film a women's retreat with fantastic speakers. All the women in the first retreat are leaders in their own right. Each of these women come from different denominations, are different ages, and are coming together to edify each other and lift each other up, share information, listen to our speakers, have a concert, and laugh and cry.

There are fun segments as well—it's not all about hard healing. It's about sharing, getting back to hospitality, and cooking. It's just going to be an absolute celebration of women. It is an encouragement to women to deal with some of those tough issues so they can be all that they can be in Christ. Since you can't give what you don't have, we want to give information they need because God wants to help women be released from their hard issues.

Wright

That sounds great. Jennifer, I know movie stars grow up like the rest of us "normal" people, and you are the person you are today because of the women who loved you as a young person. Will you tell us about the remarkable women in your life and perhaps how they influenced you in your early years?

O'Neill

That is such a wonderful question. I'd love to start with my mom. I've had my times, as many women do, with some of the areas we want to smooth out between mom and daughter. We seem to go through various cycles. I always asked the women on my television show this question, "Is it a compliment when somebody says you're just like your mom, or is it an insult?"

I have gleaned so much wonderful information and style from my mom. She is a lady to the nth degree. She was born in London. She's an extremely loyal, reliable, beautiful, elegant individual. If I have any twirl with a pen or the written word it's probably because she insisted that I develop my skills in communication. That was a great gift. I love her dearly.

Then there was my Aunt Eleanor, who I must say, in many ways I was, during certain stages of my life, closer to than to my mom because she was more playful. I missed that with my mom. Ellie would play cards with me or go out and help me with my little rock garden. She seemed to embrace my love of animals, which was foreign to my parents because they didn't know it growing up. She encouraged me. She had a piano and she encouraged me to play the piano and write and be expressive.

I remember as a young girl, when my parents would have a party, I would go twirling into the middle of the party dancing and leaping about. Ellie would always applaud and encourage my behavior. I don't know how it was received by anyone else, but just pleasing my aunt was fine. She encouraged me to express myself and upon her death, she left me her piano, which I've had with me for so many years. She also was a very godly woman. Although I didn't have any formal upbringing in the church, Ellie personified Christ who lived in her. If she had any influence, at the top of the list of the influences, I would say that she inspired me to be like her in that sense.

What was it in her that was different? What was it that gave her patience that no one else seemed to have, a compassion that no one else seemed to have? She had a heart just as big as the outdoors. When I came, very late in my life, to my belief and faith in Jesus Christ, I recognized that's what she gave me. She was just a faithful, godly, wonderful woman who planted in me a seed of her presence and her personality and her heart that I desired and aspired to.

I remember another lady, Mrs. Leone. I still remember her name. I think she was my fifth grade teacher. Some of the events in my life were born of the fact that I felt somewhat invisible and unlovable for various reasons. Early on I thought I needed to earn love. I didn't realize it was a free gift and unconditional. I didn't know because I didn't have my faith. I thought that if I got straight A's in school that my parents would love me and I would get their attention. It's a very basic and interesting view.

If we see bruises on a child's face or they're not fed, we know they're an SOS there and they need help. Many times the bruises that we carry through life through a negative impression are on our hearts. You can't see them, but you see the result of them—the hurt.

Well, with all that said, I was just determined to get straight A's in school, and in those days there were about fourteen marks. I had straight A's for all the three-year terms, except one B in spelling. In fact, I can't spell to this day. But this lady—this wonderful teacher—gave me an A in spelling. She wrote a note to my parents and said, "It's not that I'm saying that Jennifer's spelling is up to snuff and I would give an A for her actual talent in that area, but I've never seen any person want straight A's more than Jennifer does. So I'm going to give her an A for effort." That was wonderful because she instilled in me the idea to forge ahead.

If you're not naturally gifted in a certain area but you want to conquer that area—you want to become accepted for whatever reason—keep trying, keep going. If nothing else, you will be rewarded or recognized for your effort. Never give up. That's what she taught me.

Wright
She would be proud today to know that you've become a well-read person and also an author.

O'Neill
Thank God for spell-check!

Wright
Were there any famous women authors or public figures who influenced you as a young person or later in your life?

O'Neill
Yes, Margaret Meade. I was attending private school in New York and believe it or not, she came for an assembly meeting. She was such a great anthropologist. That ignited an interest in me about the world.

I never meet Helen Keller, but she was certainly a positive influence. There are so many women, if you start going through history. It's rather endless.

Wright
I probably should have asked this earlier in the interview, but I've saved the question until now for a specific reason. What do you think makes a woman remarkable?

O'Neill

Women are remarkable in such a wide variety of areas because they have such an array of talents. I would say it would be their ability to accept others in an inspirational and nurturing fashion. Whether an artist or a mother, women have a communication and caring level in them that is unique only to women. It is different than men. I think those that excel remain in touch with those parts of their femininity and are extremely effective. Those are extraordinary women to me—remarkable women are women who have not lost the idea that they're women. They do not have to conquer something.

Here's an analogy. My ex-husband used to be a rodeo cowboy. When I train a horse, my desire is to become a partner with that horse. It's an extraordinary match when it's right—when you're flying through the air (hopefully with the greatest of ease). That big animal desires to please you, is guided by just the lightest touch of your finger or your leg. It's just wonderfully elegant. My ex-husband would want to conquer the horse. He would want to "break" the horse. There's a difference. So he used to laugh at me and say, "You take ten times longer to break that horse than I do." But that was my approach.

What I admire about women is there is that soft touch, that incredible effectiveness, never losing their gentle touch.

Wright

Based on your description, which I agree with whole heartedly, many people would consider Jennifer O'Neill a remarkable woman. And I know you're not looking for a compliment.

O'Neill

I'm just trying to learn.

Wright

I know you to be a very humble person, but I would like to pursue some of the circumstances in your life that caused you to stretch and to grow, to endure and to overcome. I know our readers would be encouraged. If you don't mind, would you relate a story or two about how you have overcome some of the challenges in your life?

O'Neill

Well, for a very long time I wasn't overcoming very well. I almost died three times. I was shot and I had nine miscarriages along the way to having my three children. I was bumping into life very hard. I also broke my neck and back riding horses. But that's why I wrote my first book, *Surviving Myself,* because quite often we get in our own way. Those stumbling blocks in life—those tough ones in my case, such as being able to address my abortion as so many others who have had abortions—carried through my life and that negative feeling grew.

On the other side was the fame and fortune, traveling the world, working in Paris at age fifteen by myself, and all that a life in the public and fast lane could bring. During all that I had this hole in my heart. When I said earlier that God turns all things for good, He has used all those hard times for me to be able to say experience overrides theory.

When I started to really come into my own, my life wasn't a runaway train. I always had enormous drive. I like that about myself, but I realize now as I look back that it had a bit of frenetic tilt to it. I was tenacious on one hand and very shy on the other. What put it all together for me was my faith. It had to start with some very deep healing of those areas and accepting that someone, namely God, could actually love me and care about me, that He knew every hair on my head. He knew me before the creation of time and He knit me together in my mother's womb. He had a plan for me that was bigger than anything I could ever imagine. So talk about inspiration, that's a pretty exciting release. Not only did I receive eternal life, but it took me a good ten years to begin to accept what has always been a free gift from Christ—His love and His protection. The Holy Spirit isn't just a hospital, He's an army to engage. I had to accept that I could achieve anything that He set me on a path to do.

When I finally gave up "me" and realized that if I had any talents they were gifts from God, I wanted to use them for His glory. It was as if a floodgate had opened. We're all a work in progress, but I can begin to see the light at the end of the tunnel, and it's *not* a train! I saw how He used my movies so I'd know how to put together the *Living Forever* television series to edify women and share the good news.

Anything that I do I just give all the glory and honor to God because I wouldn't be here if I hadn't found Him. I had to stop looking down at all the stumbling blocks that I'd put in front of me or others had.

At the end of the day we're all responsible for everything we think, say, and do. When I finally got over myself—a daily laying down of bad tendencies and just asking God to come and fill me up with the

Holy Spirit and be available to Him—my life just transformed. I am excited every day. Words come out of my mouth that are from the Word, *"This is the day that the Lord has made and I will be glad in it."* A lot of the tortures that I went through were self-inflicted. It's changing your mind about how you perceive reality.

I have had a good marriage. My husband is a godly man. He's not perfect, I'm not perfect, but he has not been placed on the earth to make me happy. My happiness, my fulfillment, my satisfaction, and my peace come from my relationship with Jesus. I take advantage, if you will, of all His incredible offers to me, like dying on the cross for my sins. I accepted that finally—it's for all my sins. It's for everyone's sins.

When I finally accepted that I wasn't bound to my past through regrets, shame, pain, and all those secret places that we're so good at hiding and shoving under the carpet, I realized the truth really does make you free. When I accepted His grace, I started to heal. Now, I'm a better mom, I'm a better wife. I go into those relationships thinking what can I do for my husband and then I give him to God. I was a control freak because I was afraid of rejection and hurt, most of which I had invited into my life myself through lack of discernment and not having a solid foundation. All of that is changing and it's exciting for me.

Wright

I can understand why it would take you years. When you consider grace, forgiveness, eternal life, it's almost so overwhelming that it seems too good to be true.

O'Neill

Exactly, but it *isn't* too good to be true—God is true. I came to my faith at thirty-eight and it took some time before I really allowed myself to accept His grace.

Wright

Today's modern women must deal with countless challenges from the workplace and at home. In your opinion, what are two or three of the most critical issues facing women today and what advice would you offer women regarding these issues?

O'Neill

In my show I call it "the balancing act." Today, women's plates are so full. You just said it in the question. In the workplace or at home, we're torn. There's not a better job or a more important job than raising children and being a good wife and mom. Yet, we want to expand our territories and be all we can be. It's that balancing act that quite often seems to be a runaway train. And in its wake, what's left are broken relationships.

I also say in my show, "You turn around in bed and you look at your husband and say, 'Who are you and how did you get here?'" I think our relationships suffer because of the complexities of life. Also, we lose the knack of getting along in our marital relationships. I can only speak of this because I'm the worst offender. I finally began trying to figure it out. As I said before, I focus on changing myself and letting God do a work in my husband. Communication is the key and the fact that there are really no surprises.

Married women reach a point in their marriage when they'll say, "I don't recognize you," or "How did I ever get involved with you?" The fact of the matter is that most of the problems we have after the perfect dating stage were evident in the beginning, but we just choose not to look at the problems or we whitewash them thinking everything will be fine. Then we deal with them in our relationship later. I think those are difficult areas to balance.

One thing that might be off the question but I'd like to bring up is, I think women are confused. I think men and women have become confused about their roles over the last generation. It does not bode well for solid family living. I see the desire of families to get back to that balance. We were designed a certain way. Again, I can speak of this because I was always an independent woman who made a very good living and had a lot of exposure in life.

Celebrity, if you will, is not about getting a table at a restaurant, but for me, it allows me to have a platform for God's Word. During those years of imbalance, I didn't choose men who were terribly dynamic. Maybe it was a protective thing on my part. So I was in the driver's seat, financially and power wise. I don't say that with any kind of intent other than to state a fact. I was a very emotionally needy individual. That's not an attractive picture.

When I started to come into my faith and really understand the Word of God and the authority of His ultimate Word on how He designed us to be as man and wife, I realized that's how it has to work. We wives need to acquiesce to our husband as a man. That's difficult for women sometimes because their men, quite often, are not acting like God describes in the Bible a man (husband) should act. There's nothing wrong to listening to a man who, according to the Bible, would lay his life down for his wife and treat her like Jesus treats the church. Men love to be there, but when wives want to open our own door and make our own decisions, that strips our husbands of that. At the same time it strips us of that wonderful feeling of being able to fall into our husband's arms and feel safe and protected yet still have our own identity. He would want us to be the best we can be. I think that's gotten very confusing.

Women have confused the issues. The nth degree is the subject that I talk about all the time, such as abortion, where somehow society has managed to convince women that they have lost some inalienable right if they don't have the right to kill their own child. Something is terribly wrong with what one would call independence. By the way, the early feminists were all pro-life, which is so interesting to me. They were all pro-life. They just wanted the right to vote and they wanted the right to own their own property. They did not want a right to abort their children. So there's been a big mix-up, I think, in the feminist movement. The roles are confused and I think it's caused a lot of problems.

Wright

I think it confuses men. I know I'm confused by the confusion. It doesn't take a rocket scientist to figure out that we're different. I don't understand the unisex thought that all of us should be the same.

O'Neill

It's so wrong and it's led the family and society down a very slippery slope. It doesn't work. I love to tell this to kids when I go to schools and talk about abstinence. Again, I'm the worst offender, but I also tell people that God is so gracious. I remind people—I don't tell them—that God is so gracious with us that when that negative tape, that little voice says, "You're not worthy. You're not lovable. Who are you to stand up and talk to anybody?" (I hear that every morning when I get up and then I just rebuke it). God has given us example after example of people He's used in a powerful way, people who were just as imperfect as we are. Moses was a murderer and stuttered, and didn't want the job. The Apostle Paul called himself the worst offender—at one time he was killing Christians. Peter denied Christ. Whenever I feel that I'm infallible I just remember Peter. We need God's grace every step of the way. I think that we can all be used in a way that we cannot even imagine if we would allow Him to work in us.

Back to your question, I was talking about the kids. I get to go to schools and talk about abstinence. I give them this illustration, David, I tell them to just think for a moment that we are God's design and when God refers to being abstinent until marriage, do you have any idea why, and what the thinking is behind that? It is because He loves us. If you believe that God created us, out of all of His creations—animals and plants, etc.—only people are designed anatomically to face each other when they make love. What would that be about? It is about intimacy and trust and looking into each other's eyes. What is trust but commitment? You can't trust somebody not to leave if they are not committed. What is commitment but marriage? God designed us to be with one another in a trusting, committed fashion. Read the Song of Solomon. God designed sex, but He designed it to be enjoyed under circumstances that won't hurt us. Today, I see healing happening and relationships coming together again. By getting in the right relationship with God, the trickle-down effect is wonderful as we're starting to heal.

Wright

Jennifer, you know, you're one of my favorite people. I just love to talk with you. I always want to go on and on forever. I always learn so much when I talk with you.

When you were describing your mother I was thinking, she's describing herself because you are certainly a class act.

O'Neill

Then just a little bit of her wonder rubbed off on me, and I thank her.

Wright

Today we have been talking with Jennifer O'Neill. It's been my sincere pleasure to speak with her. She's a television and film star, but to those who know her well, she is much, much more.

Jennifer, thank you so much for sharing your heart and soul with our readers today.

O'Neill

It's such a pleasure for me to be a part of this project. I will pray God's blessings on it because women need to read about other wonderful women. We're all wonderful and we're all wonderfully made. It's just a super project!

JENNIFER O'NEILL is by far one of the world's most beautiful Hollywood film stars of all time. She started her international modeling career at the age of fifteen. She then became a film star in some of Hollywood's most bankable films like *Rio Lobo* (with John Wayne) and the award-winning classic film *The Summer of '42* (this movie made Jennifer a household name). Jennifer held a thirty-year position as spokeswomen for Cover Girl Cosmetics. Jennifer is also an animal activist, she races, trains, and breeds show horses, and is an advocate for charitable causes like the American Cancer Society and women's issues. Jennifer's career has been a dream come true, but her life was a nightmare of broken marriages, near death experiences, emptiness, abuse, and even her daughter being sexually abused by one of O'Neill's husbands. She turned her life around by becoming a born-again Christian and now ministers to hurting people worldwide through seminars and her books. Jennifer's books have won critical acclaim and her seminars are attended by millions. Jennifer is an amazing lady, a mother of three children and a grandmother. She's a survivor and has become a role model to all who hear her story.

Jennifer O'Neill
Jennifer O'Neill Ministries
Leah Persell, Executive Assistant
1811 Beech Ave.
Nashville, TN 37203
Phone: 615.463.3126
Fax: 615.463.3032
E-mail: jenniferoneill@bellsouth.net

Terri Girardi

Most women born in the 1950s or 1960s probably relate to the typical expectations of the era. We were spreading our wings a bit in college and careers, but marriage and family were a key measure of value and a great deal of childhood was spent preparing for it. Often, issues about faith were merely part of the era's social expectations as they were restricted to church attendance, potluck suppers, or the occasional bake sale or bazaar. *"You've come a long way, baby,"* was a popular marketing phrase then but many of us can relate to "coming a long way" through a transformation of faith in spite of superficial cultural expectations.

When invited to participate in *Amazing Faith*, I must admit that I was more than a little intimidated by such a lofty book title! But, it's a privilege to be included in this particular topic as I share my amazing *journey* of faith with you! Bear with me as I begin to reveal how God has shaped and molded me, building His foundation of faith that was to support me though the trauma of losing a child. Sharing my past will connect you to the hope of my future as we turn back the clock.

In the midst of those *blossoming of self* trends, actually, I grew up pretty shy without much self-confidence. As I read over my chapter biography, it's hard to imagine that my diverse list of ministries and careers grew out of that past. It's like a completely different life is playing on an eight millimeter film reel and I don't recognize the part I played then. And literally, it is a different life now.

Those early insecurities kept me from doing many things I might have accomplished when I was younger. My family was very social and as my father became more successful in the real estate business, I had many opportunities to travel and experience an adult world. As an only child, I tagged along with them to mostly adult events so I didn't relate to other children very well. I hadn't learned to appreciate it yet or see its potential, but what child appreciates something that helps them to grow?

Church life for us became a social event as well. I didn't grasp the significance of faith and I don't remember hearing about what it meant to be a Christian. Our lives were completely separate from faith issues except on the occasional Sunday morning, but seeds of faith were planted.

Most people would believe that since we attended church services, we were a Christian family. That's not really true. As a parent, I know I try to do the best job I know how and will fall short. And I know that my parents did the best they knew how. I had a wonderful relationship with both of them. So even though I was not surrounded with the knowledge of Christ, I believe that everything in my path of faith brought me to a point of decision, and they were an important part of that process. I can look back and see how God used people and circumstances to draw me.

After I was married and had two young children, I realized that I had within my reach just about everything I had dreamed about. I had earned a college degree in Marketing and was working part time in my field. I married my college sweetheart, Walt, a great looking guy who had a good job. I had one of each—a little blonde boy, and a brown-haired baby girl. Walt built a nice home for us in a rural area between two busy cities, so I enjoyed both country and city life. Culturally, I had *"arrived"* so to speak.

And wouldn't you think I would be content? But, I wasn't. I don't think I gave much thought to where real contentment could be found. I had been introduced to religion, per se, especially what I might call, "traditional middle-American religion." In many ways, though, I avoided thinking about much of anything with substance. In my early teens, our family stopped attending church services, so I no longer had a consistent point of reference. The whole idea of "religion" became a bit of a fairy tale. Maybe like, "once upon a time there was God. And He looked down on the world where He grew trees and made people and animals. And then a little baby named, Jesus, was born in a manger. And the animals were there, too. The end."

I turned down any invitations to go to church with friends because deep inside, I don't think I wanted to make any decisions about it. I

even avoided going to funerals. The fairy tale seemed to satisfy me –
why shatter traditional images like Santa Claus, the Easter Bunny,
and Jesus?

My husband and I went to his church each week as part of our
routine, but neither of us grasped its relevancy. During that process,
my cousin, Diana, invited me to a Bible study she attended. True to
form, I politely declined . . . and declined . . . and declined. There
comes a time, however, when it seems easier to accept then to keep
being asked, so I went with her under silent protest.

Well, I thought these women were all crazy! They read the Bible
and seemed to understand what it meant. They gathered around a
piano in the living room and sang these little choruses with lyrics
that sounded like some of the verses we read. And *then*, they took
turns praying out loud! I had never experienced anything like it. I felt
like a fish out of water, and was *more* than uncomfortable. Looking
back, I think I was jealous that they were able to express their faith
in a more practical and tangible way. I went again (believe it or not)
because I really did want what they had.

Several weeks or maybe months later, around Easter, I found myself alone one evening. I don't remember how that was possible, with
a young family at home, but I was alone—or so I thought. I had been
watching television in the living room, flipping through the stations.
The vivid picture of what I saw "between channels" still rests dramatically in the front of my brain. Portraying Jesus, Robert Powell,
the actor from the movie, *Jesus of Nazareth,* was hanging on the
cross in agony, blood dripping from his brow, and the shadows of the
clouds overhead shaded his face. An amazing thing happened as air
waves and images seized my attention. I heard God's voice for the
first time within me, very clear, and very confrontational.

"Jesus is either who He said He is or he isn't. Make a decision."

You can imagine how overwhelming that was. I began to weep and
in my heart—that center of who I really am; I made a decision that
night that Jesus *is* who *He* said He is. No more fairy tales. I sure
couldn't ignore this, although I didn't really understand what had
happened yet. A different life had begun. All I know is that I couldn't
read enough of the Bible. I was so thirsty to learn more about who
Jesus is and what more God had to say to me. I never imagined He
would have said anything! I watched other Christian programs. I'm
so grateful for Christian television, needless to say, and I grew rap-
idly. But I wasn't sure what to *do* with what I learned.

To say I had a different perspective on church and life from that point would be putting it mildly. But now my husband thought I was the crazy woman. God led me to ask Walt many questions. He was frustrated with my "overnight" transformation into something he really didn't recognize, but I think he was even more frustrated that he couldn't answer my questions. He had been directly involved in worship ceremonies since he was in elementary school, but he couldn't come to terms now with not knowing the foundations of the Bible or what faith really meant.

During that time I had searched out Christian events in our community that I could attend and one day in particular, I couldn't find anyone to attend with me. In another one of those miraculous moments when you can hear God's prompting without audible words, He asked, "Why don't you take the person you most care about going with you?"

I knew Walt wouldn't go with me, didn't I? He wasn't interested in going to any activity that had to do with religion except to our current church, and he certainly wouldn't encourage me to go. But with little steps forward in faith, I did ask him. And he went! And, through an incredible program of skits confronting us with faith and eternity, he accepted the reality of Christ's death and resurrection for himself and received Christ's gift of salvation that night. More crying and more growing. Both our lives, and the lives of our children, began to change in a marvelous and propelling ways.

One of our first steps was to choose a church that met us both on a common ground. As I read more and more of God's Word, and learned from other Christians, I discovered that God is able to empower us to accomplish greater things. When our children were at the Vacation Bible School age, I volunteered to help. I think I blew away the other volunteers with my exuberance to serve. How did they put up with me? It reminds me a bit of the Road Runner cartoon where he leaves everything in a cloud of dust!

I loved music and it seemed to touch my heart in a way nothing else did, so I also volunteered for music ministries. As I began to step out, Christ's strength in me became more evident and I was able to balance my inadequacies with God's work in and through me. I learned about spiritual gifts and explored using them. It helped me to become more defined and the "cloud of dust" was not quite as distracting! I'm a visionary and a planner so it excited me to try new things and watch God work. When I match that with more discipline, I might even get things done!

Eventually, I started sharing what I was learning from personal

Bible study with other women in a home-based study. I was the most experienced, even at that point, so I became the class leader. Before I knew it, my "Bible study cousin" invited me to speak at her church's women's group, which I accepted without hesitation this time. I read my entire message right off the pages, but it became a turning point for my ministry. I found that I thrived on sharing God's Word with women, both in a Bible study setting and through women's events and retreats.

I crashed and burned several times throughout my growing stages—mostly from trying to outrun God. Take my word for it: *following* Him is His perfect plan. Through the valleys of ministry, I noticed that although local churches had good programs in place for outreach and basic discipleship, there were few opportunities for women in leadership to learn more and to refresh their faith and purpose.

The Lord was planting the idea for what was to become Anathallo Women's Ministry. What kind of a ministry name is that? Let me give you some background. Over the years as a Christian, I had the privilege of studying under a wonderful Bible study teacher, Pastor Dick Budden. He took our ongoing Wednesday night class through scripture word by word. I remember it took us over five weeks to study *one* verse from Genesis! For more than twelve years he helped me appreciate digging deep into God's Word to discover its realities. Context, history, culture, and language were tools to see these truths and *understand* them! He helped me prepare to start writing and leading other studies. Walt and I led several studies together, and still do, as we're able. Through our growing ministries and through attending other churches as we grew, we met other Christians who wanted to study and learn with us.

When my vision for a women's ministry first took root in my heart, I called Pastor Dick and asked him if he knew a word that would describe this vision. I wanted to help lead a ministry that would touch the lives of women from all different backgrounds, especially women who led ministries in their home churches. It had to be a purposeful event that used time wisely and could be an opportunity not only to grow in faith and ministry, but also to refresh and renew. The word, *Anathallo,* is a Greek word meaning just that—"to renew, refresh, or bloom again." In fact, its picture word is of a fading flower that comes back to life.

This regional ministry's goal is to network with other Christian women who desire to serve God more effectively in their homes, churches, and careers. Speakers and teachers who have a passion to share their faith experiences and ministry specialties challenge us to set our roots deeply in God's Word. We leave each event better connected to the Body of Christ as a whole and with a realization that we are all in ministry twenty-four hours a day. We need each other and we need to be more readily equipped to go wherever God leads.

Seeing God's direction for our lives and learning to walk in faith is a life-long process. But I've learned to recognize God's specific voice more and more and to apply His wisdom and direction as He leads. Each time we've been faced with a career change or an opportunity to add a new facet to what we already do, God has set a clear path.

Oh, I didn't always recognize the path! I still don't. It's very easy for me to be distracted by the day-to-day. The world's voice is very loud. And a busy schedule can cloud your heart and mind with too many distractions. Women today have filled just about every second. But God continues to use those clear words or phrases with me. He surrounds me with instruction, whether it's through other people, specific scripture, or even a television show!

As Walt has developed into a strong, spiritual leader with his own gifts and insight, we blend our faith and walk forward together. It's a reflection of what marriage is about—being equally yoked with the common goal of working together to please God as 2 Corinthians describes. Because we so enjoy being with other people, and each other, our careers have combined our education and experience with the desire to be in fellowship. We have an entrepreneurial spirit so we always look for ways to use where the Lord has placed us in life to gather people around us. Every day is a new adventure. That's hard for many, but I feel as if I was created for adventure.

Recently we took the opportunity to pursue the purchase of two of the international women's fitness clubs, *Curves*, in our community. I had suffered from chronic, debilitating migraines for more than thirty-four years, and have finally taken steps to be more obedient in being a better steward of my body. Wellness is becoming a partnership with God for me, in uncovering His design for my health. I have neglected it and tried to turn over my accountability to others. Over the last few years, God had placed specific material and people in my life to help me learn more about nutrition and fitness. I began to see these principles revealed in scripture in a way I had never noticed before. I gained additional wisdom from these principles and as I studied the science of how God had created my body to work, I was empowered to make better choices. Then I wanted to share what I was learning with others.

I'm convinced that health is a subject we may purposefully neglect in the church. We're all a little put off by messages on "giving" and "finances," too. Somehow we've believed the misconception that our body, our money, and our material possessions belong exclusively to us and that God has no part in them! More often than not we're not willing to surrender to God's will in these areas or please Him by relinquishing control to the One who creates and provides! Look at the conflict that arises when we talk about subjects like our bodies in worship or in tithing issues.

Everything belongs to God, whether I'm willing to surrender or not! And thank God that they do belong to Him. I've done a pretty poor job with controlling them myself so far. And there are still so many areas of life and faith that I know I'm unwilling to surrender yet.

My new classes, "God's Design for Health & Wellness," combine challenging Bible study with applicable health and nutrition information. It's about surrender and accountability. And the format is designed around a one-evening or one daytime class to make it practical for our busy lives.

Being able to pull all the things God has done in our ministries and careers together in this way fuels my faith. And after my fiftieth birthday! (Of course now I'm thinking a lot more about my health and fifty sounds a lot younger than it used to. No matter what decade you approach, it always sounds younger than it did before, doesn't it?) But in this phase of my life, with an adult, married child, it would be tempting to slow things down a bit. I sat down one day and made a mental list of all the reasons I *shouldn't* start a new career or add a big project in addition to what we already had on our plate (excuse the nutrition pun).

I finally asked God. His response was, "Reach people." I had to admit that I couldn't reach many people from my garden or a beach chair, so God's "list" won hands down. A friend and coworker, Vicki, encouraged me in our decision by proclaiming, "Re-fire, don't re-tire!"

In the midst of constructing a new building complex that will house several of our businesses, and all the big and little details that fill the mind and day with that, I know it's all about reaching people and helping *them* reach their full potential both physically and spiritually. We were designed to learn and grow together. It's what makes me so passionate about teaching and speaking.

Passion is the key to my faith. We all have a choice about how fervently we want to know God and follow who He is in Christ, but I wonder if it's hard sometimes for me to grasp real faith without roots that go back into my childhood. So many of my friends and church family had the privilege of growing up knowing Bible stories. These stories are part of their lives and what they knew to be true. On the other hand, I might have become a Christian without some of the baggage that comes with traditional church. I didn't know I couldn't do something because "it wasn't done that way." And, I didn't hear much denominational doctrine before I heard God's Word.

I know that when I teach and lead, I study and I pray. I dig deeply into scripture, word by word, and its simple message of God's love for us is revealed in every verse in more significant ways. I begin to see more and more that the thread of these truths is woven through the entire Bible.

One of the most important things I teach when I speak or lead is that the Bible is contextual. Imagine that if we were in a local book club and the club leader took the featured book, ripped it in half, and gave each side of the room only one of the halves. Then, what if each group was asked to explain the story, its characters, plot, and outcome? How ridiculous would that be? Why did the characters act as they did? What motivated them to respond and interact? What was the point and significance of the story? Neither group would know. Oh, they'd guess and make up their own version based on only the half they had, but no one would understand the author's intent. It's only when you read the whole book that you begin to put the pieces together. The Bible in its fullness is revealed as a whole. Simple message—wonderfully complex truths.

When it comes right down to it, I think that by surrounding myself with the *realities* of scripture, of who God really is, and the *facts* of Christ, by praying and hearing God's voice, and experiencing God's kingdom for myself, I am purposefully building faith. I am deliberately transforming my mind and being led by my heart. It takes hard work, and I frequently don't feel up to the task; but it's well worth the effort. Doubt and apathy are much easier—they are certainly more natural. But doubt and apathy lead to an extremely superficial life. A plant with shallow roots wilts very quickly. That's something I *did* learn by spending time with God in my garden.

I'd like to say that building faith in my life was a consistent, natural progression of basic elements. But we all know that when faith is tested, we grow the most. It's one thing to read about kingdom principles, even teach them to others, but it's quite another thing to go through circumstances that put them into practice. There's where the reality is shown.

In the midst of growing in our faith and building our careers, a page turned in our lives that we didn't expect. Our family was out to dinner one night, celebrating Walt's forty-second birthday. We love fussing over each other for special events and holidays so it was natural for us to do something together. Our son, Tony, was starting his second semester at college, and our daughter, Sara Jean, was in high school, so I was grateful that we were still able to fit family events in our schedules.

When we got back home and got ready for bed, Tony didn't feel very well, but he'd had other days of nausea recently, so we didn't think much about it. He came upstairs from his bedroom in the basement feeling worse, so I decided to lie on the floor next to him and he transferred to the couch. I remember praying that I wanted to take his symptoms myself, so he would finally feel better. (I think many parents feel that way when their children are sick. Can you imagine how much more our Heavenly Father wants to do that for us?) But when I started feeling just as queasy and Tony wasn't feeling any better, I thought that we had probably gotten a bit of food poisoning at the restaurant. Walt took my place with Tony and I went back to bed thinking I would rest better there.

I have a vague memory of waking up in the bathroom, on the floor. I couldn't believe how sick I'd become, but I couldn't seem to respond. I managed to get up and head back toward my bed. The next thing I knew, I was on the front porch of our home with paramedics surrounding me. Walt was crying and I could hear him asking how I was. It was a bitterly cold, February night, now turned to early morning. The paramedics wrapped me in extra blankets and carried me on a stretcher to an ambulance. Everything seemed so gray. For a moment, I heard sounds like wind chimes or a child's tiny piano. The chimes turned into Sara's voice. "I'm okay, Mom," she cried out. "I'm okay, Mom," she kept calling. It was literally like music.

Then I could hear Walt's desperate voice clearer. "My son!" he cried. "Where is my son?"

It's been ten years as of the writing of this book, and I can hear everything in my head as clearly as if it were yesterday.

By now, the sun was above the horizon and I remember looking up and seeing the bare treetops from the ambulance windows. Walt was lying on a stretcher next to me. I don't think my head has ever hurt that badly, and I couldn't get warm. I was throwing up constantly.

I'm not sure at what point they explained that we had become ill from carbon monoxide poisoning. I wasn't even sure I knew what that meant. But something within me sensed that Tony was gone. Once at the hospital, I confronted a paramedic. I'm sure he wanted the news to come from someone we knew, or the hospital chaplain, so all he was able to tell us was that only three of us came to the hospital.

Tony had died from the poisoning. Whether God's strength in me became mighty at that very moment, or my brain blocked off emotion, I have to confess that I can't be sure. Either way, God was protecting me. I was able to respond to the hospital staff, to make some calls, and to concentrate on Walt and Sara Jean.

Our pastor, Larry Kiser, was the first to walk in the room. His sensitivity and strength were such a reflection of Christ's presence to us. He's been teased about crying at the drop of a hat, but admits that he has only recently grown into the ability to express his emotions honestly. We have been blessed by his example and leadership. He cares deeply about things and shows it. And having eight children of his own, the fact that he could relate to my grief was so important.

While we cried and talked and prayed, Walt was taken to another wing of the hospital to a hyperbaric chamber. His internal organs had begun to shut down and because carbon monoxide dramatically restricts the body's oxygen supply, he needed oxygen therapy as quickly as possible. The problem he was having was similar to when divers dive deep into the ocean and suffer decompression illness ("the bends") if they come back to the surface too quickly. What a picture of what we were going through! God was already lifting *us* up "from the depths of the sea." Sara Jean was released and her friends from school and a few of their parents came as soon as they were able.

A warmth and peace surrounded me in a way I will never be able to explain. Even though my physical body was still chilled, I didn't notice any more. Christ's love poured out in a visible expression of the Holy Spirit through the many people who helped us. More family members and friends came and filled that little emergency room as we waited for Walt's results. Prayers were being lifted up in all corners of the world through the miraculous new technology of cellular phones and e-mail.

As my mind cleared in the midst of the pain, I started to put the pieces of the puzzle together. When our daughter and hero, Sara Jean, woke up for school, effected only a little by the poisoning, she had called 911 after finding me unconscious, half out of bed. I can't imagine what she must have faced and the grief that gripped her when she found her dad and her brother unconscious in the living room, realizing that Tony wasn't breathing. But she had the courage to call and work with the operator until the ambulance arrived. She was such a comfort, both then and in the weeks to come, as she reassured us of her love and of the value of our parenting.

One of the *many* miracles that followed was that Walt stayed only briefly in the hospital and had no symptoms of the usual effects of poisoning after he recovered. I wish I could tell you more about the amazing things that God revealed to us and the supernatural events that surrounded us, but I think that would fill another whole book! I hope our paths cross someday in person, or through mail, so I *can* tell you more. This is so that we might *"pass on the same help and comfort that God has given us."*

Sharing our experience is one of the most important aspects of our lives, and one of the hardest, even if it's just to tell people to buy and use a carbon monoxide (CO) detector in their homes. Through our ministries and careers we have the opportunity to meet so many people, so we tell our story often. The death of our son literally carried us from knowing *about* God's love and provision to *experiencing* it firsthand. We want so much to share with others the hope of eternity and the realities of seeing God's kingdom unfold before our eyes.

Faith is trust. Everyone has faith in something! We may have faith in our spouse, or faith in our career, faith in the government, or in some form of religious ritual. We "trust" that we'll have a job when we go to work the next day. My faith was growing by reading and hearing, but it was time to *trust* God and to shift my faith from people, things, and circumstances to God's kingdom "on earth, as it is in heaven." The kingdom starts *now.*

It's hard to talk about what happened only because our hearts break again and again. The grief pours out. But God truly has comforted us so that we can comfort others. And we are able to share the realities of Christ in a way that draw others to listen. There's great hope in that, too.

The word "hope" comes from the Hebrew word *"yachal,"* meaning "to expect, trust, wait." We usually use the word "hope" pretty loosely. We will say, "I hope it doesn't rain" or "I hope we can go on vacation." But that's more like wishful thinking. The hope we have in God comes from our *expectation.* We can *expect* that God will love us, forgive us through Christ, and carry us right to His side as He promised when we leave this earth. I can *expect* God to be faithful, especially when I'm not. I can *expect* that God does not change and that His

91

Word is true. Trusting God is the beginning of faith and part of a life-long process of maturity.

No one else will experience God's care and love in the same way we were allowed to, but having our eyes opened to supernatural provision helped us understand the difference between joy *because of* trials, and joy *in spite of* trials. The Holy Spirit will teach you remarkable things when you're desperate to see them, as we were.

We needed hope. We needed to trust God. It's much easier to lose faith or to blame God, so we used all the energy we had left to listen to God's voice. Most nights I couldn't close my eyes and sleep without reliving the nightmare over and over. Walt would read to me in bed from great Christian books on heaven. Joni Eareckson Tada's book, *Heaven: Your Real Home*, helped fill our thoughts with the hope of eternity and we could finally sleep. We read and reread cards and notes from friends and family. God's soothing, caring voice was everywhere.

One of the most important lessons I learned from the Holy Spirit was that *sin* causes failure. And sin is simply being out of God's will. This world, then, will fail. Furnaces will fail, jobs will fail, relationships will fail, and bodies will fail. God *draws* us to His love and salvation so that He can help *carry* us through each trial. And sin was our choice, not His. But without choice, I couldn't choose to love God—*freely*. We will either face the result of sin in this world with God or without God. I can't even imagine how horrifying it would be to face something like this without Him. And if we choose eternity with the Father who gave us life, we will never be separated from Him—life unending.

I can't say that my faith was stable throughout the trauma. I was so angry and discouraged many times over the years that I couldn't pray, like a pouting child who refuses to talk to her parents. But God never let me get so far that I wasn't able to hear Him calling me back. A friend would drop by, I'd get a note in the mail, or a Bible verse would resound in my thoughts. And more often than not, God would simply speak to me with one of those words or phrases that would pull me back up and help me walk forward again.

I don't want the fire of faith to fade. I can't see down the path to what's coming, nor do I want to. I know there will be more trials in this world, and in my world, but Christ said that He has overcome the world. That's not a military victory—it's an *e*-ternal and *in*-ternal victory. I want to be even more prepared, with roots down even deeper.

It's also been an important part of my faith journey to realize that nothing I *do* can earn God's grace or His mercy—neither in my growing relationship with God, nor more importantly, in my salvation. How weak my attempts are in comparison to what *Christ did*—what He already accomplished in my behalf. Could I make a list of "things to do" that would be enough to earn heaven? Of course not. When I realized what Christ meant as he was dying on the cross and said, "It is finished," I finally understood that He wasn't talking about His *life* being finished, He was talking about the work and sacrifice was finished to pay the penalty for my sins. *My* sins! Christ finished that work—it was complete and perfect. And when I accept that gift, my work is to share what He did with others. Because of the cross, when the Father sees me, He sees Christ. It overwhelms me just to write it.

Then, unfortunately, my very next thought can shift from faith to feeble thinking and in trying to make some kind of "deal" with God. If I serve in that ministry, or do this job, or go to church, or help that person, maybe He'll except me or love me more. Would that qualify me better to enter heaven? It helps me to say it and write it out like this because it sounds even more impossible to me then. Are you going to heaven? You might say, "I *hope* so." That's not expectation—that's wishful thinking. My hope is in Christ's ability, not my own.

I know I'm throwing out a lot of "Christianese" terms, but I want you to know where the foundation of my faith rests. It's right back to hope and "being sure of what I cannot see." Hebrews 11:1 says it best, "Now faith is being *sure* of what we hope for and *certain* of what we do not see." (NIV, emphasis supplied.)

When I write, or speak, or teach, I'm fueling the flames that help keep my faith alive! And all this time my audiences thought it was for their benefit. ☺ I certainly hope they benefit, too. Everything we do is only the means that allows us to share what God has accomplished in and with our lives. I'm committed to teaching God's Word because through it we can discover more about who God really is and about the treasures and blessings of His Kingdom as we apply those principles to our circumstances. Whether it's through Walt's and my careers in helping people to be safe and healthy, through our bed and breakfast business where we can serve others and fellowship with them, or in each of our other ministries at home and with our families, at church, or through our studies and events, I want God's glory to be seen. That's a lofty vision too, but the attempt seems worth it.

It's a joy and privilege to be asked to speak or teach. Touching one another's lives is so significant in helping us to build faith. I hope the invitations never stop. And when someone picks up something I've written and is able to use it to learn and grow or share with someone else—I may never even know about it—it's a small way for me to help others hear God's voice, as I have.

The true test of faith in action, though, isn't necessarily in my specific ministry or career. It's when I talk to a friend or a client or business associate on the phone for longer than I planned and see it as an opportunity, not an interruption. It's when I *listen*, and really care about what others say instead of talk or when I'm driving down the highway and I let someone get in ahead of me and I smile, letting them know my Christian bumper sticker and attitude match. It's when I stop all those "important" things I'm doing to drop someone a note of encouragement and include a verse that God used to comfort and encourage *me*. It's when I stop complaining about how busy I am (as if ministry were ever a burden!). It's *sharing* faith in the everyday, isn't it? Faith is about the everyday, trusting God in the details. Everything we do is only part of the path that will take us even further. What an amazing journey of faith awaits each of us.

A wife and mother of two from southwest Michigan, Terri Girardi's ministries have ranged from inspirational speaker and author, special events planner, and Bible study teacher, to music and worship leader. Her focus has been on writing and leading in-depth Bible studies that highlight original texts through topical subjects in an interdenominational environment. Specializing in women's ministries, she celebrates the diversity and unity of the Body of Christ. An active part of Richland Bible Church, she is grateful for the support system that encourages ministry participation not only within the local foundations of corporate worship and discipleship, but "outside the four walls" where how we've grown and what we've learned are put into action.

As Founding Director of *Anathallo Women's Ministry*, a regional training ministry for Christian women, Terri invested her passion for discipleship into providing a spiritual oasis where women of all denominations might find renewal while being challenged to serve more effectively in their home, church, and careers. The ministry helps to network other Christian women by sharing their gifts and talents, pooling their resources, and benefiting from a broader ministry base.

With a degree in Marketing and pursuit of a degree in Nutrition, Terri is developing a Bible study program, "God's Design for Health & Wellness," which she leads regionally. She and her husband, Walt, find great satisfaction in working together in their mechanical engineering firm, *Girardi Consulting*, as well as in their northern Michigan Bed & Breakfast, *Breezy Isle Retreat*. Expanding their love for serving others, Walt, Terri, and their daughter, Sara Jean Benander, now own and operate two *Curves International* fitness franchises. As a result, their combined personal experiences and varied business expertise allow them to promote both physical and spiritual health. Their most recent venture is building a meeting, fitness, and health facility, *Galesburg Crossings,* in their hometown of Galesburg, Michigan.

Terri Girardi
10119 East "ML" Avenue
Galesburg, MI 49053-8724
Phone: 269.665.9397
E-mail: terri@girardiweb.com
www.girardiweb.com